P9-DZY-907

Racism
In American Education:
A Model For Change

Racism In American Education: A Model For Change

William E. Sedlacek
Glenwood C. Brooks, Jr.

Nelson-Hall   Chicago

Library of Congress Cataloging in Publication Data
Sedlacek, William E.
   Racism in American education.
   Bibliography: p.
   Includes index.
   1. Discrimination in education—United States.
2. Race Discrimination—United States.   I. Brooks,
Glenwood C., joint author.   II. Title.
LC212.2.S42   370.19′342′0973   76-6909
ISBN 0-88229-136-X (cloth)
ISBN 0-88229-585-3 (paper)

To all the people in our lives, past, present, and future, who have made us racists but, at the same time, have sown the seeds of our liberation.

Contents

Acknowledgments   ix
Foreword   xi
1   Introduction   1
2   Cultural and Racial Differences   11
3   How Racism Operates   37
4   Examining Racial Attitudes   63
5   Sources of Racial Attitudes   81
6   Changing Behavior: What Can Be Done   97
7   Changing Behavior: How It Can Be Done   107
8   The Unique Role of the Black   135
9   The Unique Role of the White   147
10   Evaluation and Final Comments   159
Appendix   179
Bibliography   205
Name Index   219
Subject Index   223

Acknowledgments

We wish to acknowledge the students, teachers, and administrators at many levels of education who have provided us opportunities to study and work with them on race-related problems. We particularly thank Ruth Bloedel, Dorothy Clark, Robert Freeman, Alan Hedman, LeRoy Nattress, Dario Prieto, E. B. Smith, and Lois Wright for their comments and suggestions on the manuscript. We also acknowledge the excellent typing and general assistance provided by Anne Morgan.

Foreword

Contrary to the theories of racist organizations such as the Ku Klux Klan and the Nazi party of pre–World War II, José Vasconcelos, a Mexican philosopher and prophet, once stated that "neither in antiquity nor in the present has there ever been a race that is self-sufficient to forge an authentic civilization. The most famous epochs have been precisely those in which various peoples of different races have come into contact and mixed."

While we are far from achieving a unified body of mixed races, a universal race, the fact that we still have to live and work together with all of our cultural differences is undeniable. Our immediate fate may be borne less painfully if we understand that oftentimes our negative attitude toward others manifests itself in fear, distrust, dislike, and anger and is due to our inability to understand and cope with that which is different from ourselves.

The authors of this book have taken into account the great number of culturally different groups in the United States and therefore do not attempt to define the specific characteristics which make each group authentically different. Most important, the intent is to reflect upon certain principles of racism and how to apply them in specific situations. Most "for instances" are based on data collected on blacks since more research has been related to this group than to other minorities. Of course, American Indians, Mexican Americans, mainland Puerto Ricans, and other minority groups have suffered comparable discrimination that has not been documented in all cases.

This work addresses itself to the major problems of individual and institutional racism—how it operates, what can be done to minimize it, and how this can be done. The principles and the resolutions of the problems of racism in this book are extremely well constructed and well documented, and can be applied to or by any racial group, individual, or institution.

Since the first civil rights days, millions of dollars, federal and private, have been poured into all types of programs designed to increase minority representation in all fields of higher education. Various types of programs have come and gone but very little has been accomplished in dealing with the deep-rooted problems of "institutional" racism.

This book provides the first sound basis for training individuals and groups in developing sensible approaches to situations resulting from feelings of racism, between individuals and groups and between institutions and minority groups.

DARIO O. PRIETO
Director, Minority Affairs
Association of American Medical Colleges

Introduction

Racism, which is measurable and operational, takes many complex forms, including some that are peculiar to education and educators. The goal of this book is to provide an approach or model for eliminating racism in education. The model has been developed over several years and is based on research and direct experience in various types and levels of educational settings. The model for change is aimed primarily at whites and/or white-oriented institutions, since whites control the bulk of the educational system.

The book will deal with the model stage by stage, demonstrating its utility with examples in a number of school, college, and university settings. We feel that a systematic and pragmatic approach is needed in an area where well-intentioned but unsystematic efforts have often met with failure. The model for change provides for flexibility, but always with a goal in mind.

While the model can be applied in many different circumstances, this book will present it in the context of a workshop or conference, which is a common format in educational training. While such workshops can take many forms, a typical organization has both small group discussions or work sessions and large group sessions where information and small-group progress are shared. There also would be one consultant for every fifteen or twenty participants. More information about implementing the model will be supplied throughout the book, particularly in Chapter 7.

A number of major principles are incorporated in this approach to racism. First, it is outcome oriented, or what we will call "behavioral." That is, the emphasis is on the results of actions rather than on the actions themselves. Indeed, we define racism in terms of outcomes or behaviors. One trap that is regularly encountered by many who attempt to effect change is to be overly concerned with process or method instead of with well-specified goals. In other words, people become involved with *how* to effect change without knowing exactly *what* they are trying to accomplish.

A second characteristic of the model for effecting change is the inclusion of monitoring methods at each stage. This, obviously, is closely tied to the outcomes. In addition to results, we need some way to assess or evaluate them. Thus our model provides evaluations of short-term, intermediate, and long-term goals in eliminating racism.

Third, the suggested procedures are progressive; that is, one must work through the various stages sequentially, building on each earlier stage. In this sense, our suggestions reflect Maslow's (1954) hierarchy of needs: individuals or institutions are unwilling, or perhaps unable, to move to a more advanced stage unless the outcomes for earlier stages have been accomplished. The early stages of this model for change deal with disseminating information about cultural and racial differences and racism; the later stages deal with goals and strategies.

Fourth, the suggestions in our model should be applied so as to provide minimum discomfort to the people or institutions one is attempting to change. Shocking people may make it more difficult to reach or communicate with them. Thus the necessity of moving people through the model should be kept in mind, and whatever will facilitate such movement should be employed. Although the purpose is not to deliberately provoke others, a successful implementation of the model will probably result in shaking up the values, perceptions, and ideas of many people. Change always incorporates discomfort and doubt (Toffler, 1970). In fact, one intermediate criterion for measuring the success of the model is whether people are thinking new thoughts and expressing or acting out doubts about their present behavior.

Some critics might say that our approach is negative because it forces people to deal with unpleasant reality before designing strategies for change. Hence they may "turn off" before they reach the final, critical stages. While this is a risk, it is necessary to move through the early stages before discussing strategies. Most people have developed an elaborate and comfortable set of rationalizations around a denial of the problems or even the existence of racism. It would be useless to discuss strategies for solving a problem people do not feel exists.

Ideally, the model will deal with people at the stage where they are. Thus if a person were aware of racial and cultural differences, and the operational existence of racism, and had been confronted with and understood his or her own racial attitudes, he or she would be ready to discuss goals and strategies. However, since our model for change is applied to groups or institutions, it is obvious that all people are not at the same stage of awareness. We have consistently found that few people or institutions are immediately ready for real change, but certain individuals are often quite willing to help the group move forward. In fact the active involvement of participants is an important strategy for the "change agent." (We define a change agent as someone who accomplishes systematic social change through his or her actions.) Additionally, it is quite likely that key people, who control an institution, should be approached first and independently, because they may be at different stages from one another and from the rank and file.

We have repeatedly found that if the earlier stages of disseminating information are ignored or insufficiently covered, participants will tend to go back to a stage where they were comfortable. Most people categorically resist changes of any kind. Another problem in working with groups occurs when there is too much time between sessions. A group, or the individuals in it, may regress to an earlier stage between sessions. Thus for many people the model for change must be continually restated and worked through. When time is very short, a change agent should be more direct in trying to influence the group. Lectures and prepared materials and summaries may be called for. Generally, with more time, it is advisable to draw people out and let them reach for themselves the conclusions you are leading them toward. However, whether the total time one has to work with a person or group is an hour or a number of years, the stages in the model should be covered in consecutive order.

Another important principle is that minority and majority group members (e.g., blacks and whites) must participate as change agents or consultants. There are many important and well-differentiated roles for both minority and majority consultants to play. Specific strategies and principles for majority and minority consultants will be discussed throughout this book. A summary of the stages and the critical points follows.

STAGE I: CULTURAL AND RACIAL DIFFERENCES

Key Points to Be Understood (1) Cultural and racial differences exist, and they should be openly discussed and understood by all. (2) Differences should be approached and presented positively, in and out of the classroom. (3) Expressions of racial and cultural identity are necessary and healthy for cultural and racial minorities, and also for the rest of society. (4) "Standard English" is the white middle-class dialect, but teachers and pupils should be allowed cultural expression through other dialects, even in the classroom. (5) Many students from cultural and racial minority groups have questionable environmental support for education and are not likely to be motivated by traditional methods. (6) Minority students may act differently from whites, and may generally react more negatively to authority in a society they feel has oppressed them. (7) Most white teachers are not prepared by background or training to work with minority students. (8) The characteristics associated with cultural-racial groups are dynamic rather than static. (9) Understanding cultural and racial differences and designing appropriate educational experiences, and reinforcing that context, are crucial to any educational system.

STAGE II: HOW RACISM OPERATES

Key Points to Be Understood (1) *Individual* racism is an action taken by one individual toward another, which *results in negative outcomes,* because the other person is identified with a certain group. The group may be racial, cultural, sexual, ideological, etc. (2) *Institutional* racism is action taken by a social system or institution which *results in nega-*

tive outcomes for members of a certain group or groups. (3) These definitions of racism are *behavioral,* in that *results, not intentions, are important.* Most racism is unknowing or unintentional. (4) Those who have power to influence others, whether or not they are in the numerical majority, are the primary perpetuators of racism. (5) Since most of this society is run by and for whites, racism is primarily a white problem. Unless whites are able to change individually and collectively through their institutions, white racism is likely to remain.

Some examples of racism that are commonly found in elementary and secondary school levels are: (1) Segregated systems keep blacks isolated in geographical pockets, which results in fewer facilities, fewer teachers, and less money spent per pupil. (2) Because supervisors are poorly prepared and perhaps uncomfortable in dealing with teachers and problems in primarily black schools, they tend to make fewer visits to these schools. (3) There are few minority people in supervisory or central staff positions in most schools. (4) Most elementary and secondary school curricula are oriented toward white middle-class children. (5) Curriculum materials that are relevant to blacks and other minorities are now available but are little used. (6) Schools allocate insufficient funds and personnel for work on race relations.

Further examples, in higher education, are: (1) Biased admission standards result in fewer minority students on the nation's campuses. (2) Faculty members have low expectations of minority student performance. (3) Most student activities are organized primarily for whites. (4) Most counselors are not knowledgeable about minority students' problems and concerns. (5) There are only limited course offerings that are relevant to minority students. (6) Few minority personnel are in key decision-making roles. (7) Programs for minority students tend to be understaffed and underfunded. (8) Schools commit little of their own funds to minority student programs.

Racism is analogous to alcoholism in that one says, "Well, maybe I drink too much occasionally, but I am *not* an alcoholic!" However, only if we understand and admit our alcoholism can we begin to work on it. We are all racists and we should begin to remove that bias.

STAGE III: EXAMINING RACIAL ATTITUDES

Key Points to Be Understood (1) Most people have negative attitudes toward other races and cultural groups. (2) Racial attitudes may directly influence behavior. (3) Racial attitudes can be measured and analyzed. The Situational Attitude Scale (SAS), discussed in this book, was developed for that purpose. (4) Whites generally react more *negatively* to blacks than to whites in a personal or social situation. (5) Whites react more *positively* to blacks than to whites in a service role. (6) The referents "Negro" and "black" evoke similar reactions from whites. (7) There is a strong "social set" among whites to appear to react favorably to blacks. (8) Whites' attitudes toward blacks must be measured in a racial context; otherwise they can be successfully masked. (9) Racial attitudes as measured by the SAS have a direct relationship to dogmatic and authoritarian attitudes. (10) White females tend to react particularly negatively to sexual or physical contact with black males.

STAGE IV: SOURCES OF RACIAL ATTITUDES

Key Points to Be Understood (1) We all hold racial stereotypes that determine how we feel and act toward other races. (2) Textbooks help perpetuate racial stereotypes. (3) The nature of prejudice and racism should be taught at all educational levels. This is particularly crucial for young whites because they are not likely to avoid becoming racists without help. (4) Direct study of prejudice and racism, as well as studies that are relevant to minority cultures, should be an integral part of the regular curriculum and should not be isolated as a one-occasion experience. (5) One reason why racial stereotypes are institutionalized is that teachers, both minority and white, tend to expect less from minority students. (6) Since we have defined racism and seen that our attitudes are negative, let's assume that racism exists and see what we can do about it.

STAGE V: CHANGING BEHAVIOR: WHAT CAN BE DONE?

Key Points to Be Understood (1) Goals must be stated so as to provide directions for change. (2) Goals should be as specific and operational as possible. (3) Strategies are separate from goals in that they are ways of accomplishing goals. (4) Goals must be adjusted to the context of the times. (5) All goals must be evaluated as to the extent of their accomplishment.

Some examples of goals that were derived from applications of the model are: (1) Change the concept of teacher quotas and develop a fair policy. (2) Integrate minority- and racism-related content into the curriculum. (3) Instigate more effective preplanning and programming in newly desegregated schools. (4) Eliminate inappropriate discipline. (5) Change the use of standardized test scores. (6) Find ways of involving minority students' parents in school affairs. (7) Make sure there is follow-up after a conference or workshop. (8) Develop proper techniques for teaching standard English to black youngsters. Make sure that customary speech mannerisms are not "put down" in the process. (9) Achieve central administration support for positions that are taken to reduce or eliminate racism. (10) Find appropriate standards for judging and developing programs for blacks in a positive way. (11) Experience and understanding of racism and race relations should be required of all school personnel. (12) Black artists and scholars should be included in the curricula.

STAGE VI: CHANGING BEHAVIOR: HOW IT CAN BE DONE

Key Points to Be Understood (1) The effective change agent must be prepared for many contingencies. (2) The only test of a strategy is whether it works. (3) Most limitations to effective change are self-imposed. (4) More people are capable of affecting institutions than ever give it a try. (5) Effective action requires that a change be viewed as "moral" by its proponents. (6) Situations can be dramatized by a tactic that has no direct connection with a given goal. (7) The effective change agent is irreverent toward most social institutions. (8) Employ strategies that are unfamiliar to those one is trying to change. (9) One must always be prepared to carry out a bluff. (10) Humorous strategies are often more effective than serious ones. (11) Effective use of research data requires routine involvement with those one is trying to change. (12) The size of a group does not appear to be critical in generating change. (13) Compromise is a useful tactic. (14) One can ask for more than is wanted and settle for what was actually wanted. (15) Power can be developed by becoming the only viable source of information on a topic. (16) Power should not be used directly if this can be avoided. (17) One should select goals that can realistically be accomplished. (18) Strategies exist independently of the nature of the goal and the personality of the strategist.

Some specific strategies which were used to accomplish the goals noted above in Stage V are: (1) Get accurate counts of the number of presently employed minority teachers and go to the media and encourage positions more extreme than yours. (2) Use in-service teacher training and encourage the open treatment of racial topics as they occur. (3) Dramatize problems through the experience of others and the use of student and parent groups. Include groups other than teachers and students in your program. (4) Emphasize cultural and racial differences as they relate to discipline. (5) Encourage the use of culturally appropriate tests and measures rather than the abolishment of all tests. (6) Visit parents at home and avoid "conventional" expectations for organizational style, time of meeting, etc. (7) Set up a working structure that will monitor the change. Make long-term evaluations of progress. (8) Use professionals and the various methods cited in this section. (9) Get the facts on what is happening and know more about the operation of racism than the administrator. (10) Use the principles from Stage I: Cultural and Racial Differences. No *standards* are appropriate for everyone. (11) Use in-service training and data to dramatize points. (12) Emphasize the relatively low cost of part-time scholars and artists and the obvious benefits to majority and minority students.

2

Cultural And Racial Differences

The phrase "cultural and racial differences" represents a complex cluster of topics that gives rise to many interpretations and generates many misunderstandings. So before we go any further, the terms must be defined.

Many writers in anthropology, biology, social psychology, and related disciplines have struggled long and hard to define what is meant by "culture" and "race." For our purpose, however, a *culture* is a group of people whose members speak the same dialect and share common activities, values, and interests. *Dialect* refers to the group's common use of grammatical structures, slang, idioms, patterns of speech, etc. *Race* refers to a group which has some common biological characteristics that are relevant to the social interactions and lifestyle of that group.

In many situations it is difficult or impossible to sort

out the differences between race and culture, and two groups in the United States illustrate our point. Blacks from the United States share many forms of behavior that classify them as having a distinct culture. However, we also know that biological variables, relating to skin color, and a variety of physical characteristics make blacks in the U.S. a biological or racial group as well. A second group in the United States that is both culturally and biologically defined is Jews. Many cultural forms of behaviors have developed among Jews, centering on religion, education, and common experiences as immigrants or common lifestyles developed in other countries and brought here and handed down. At the same time, many Jews share a common biological background, having the physical characteristics of Semites.

We also recognize that many black and Jewish cultural or racial subgroups also meet these definitions.

Whether a given action or behavior is biological or cultural in origin, or arises from some combination, will not be a concern in this book. We are concerned with identifiable and observable behaviors exhibited by a group, regardless of origin, that differentiate it from other groups. We will use the term "cultural-racial" to describe such groups. We are also aware that there are an almost infinite number of groups that could be called cultural-racial. But since this book is about racism, we will concentrate on cultural-racial groups which are discriminated against in the United States—blacks, Chicanos, and native Americans or American Indians. We will describe the dynamics of racism in the next chapter.

Our purpose here is to explore cultural and racial differences as a prerequisite to understanding racism. We will illustrate our points with examples relating to blacks and other cultural-racial groups, but we hope readers will apply these ideas to any group that is discriminated against in society.

Cultural-racial groups change and evolve, but the points we are trying to make remain.

Thus far cultural-racial groups have been presented from the perspective of the people within those groups. An issue that makes the entire topic much more complex, however, is how minority cultural-racial groups are defined by the majority groups that control and influence their lives. Do blacks represent the same kind of cultural-racial group to whites as they do to themselves? The answer appears to be no. To illustrate this point, Golden (1958) presented an interesting description of the travels of a black man through the South, posing as a potentate from a Middle-East country. He was treated royally, even though many of his characteristics, physical and otherwise, were similar to those of many local blacks. Conversely, we know of a student from Afghanistan who had dark skin but no other Negroid features and was constantly surprised by the reactions he received from whites. Some considered him a black, some a foreigner, and still others treated him as a white.

The point is that *the operational definition of a minority cultural-racial group consists not only of the cultural perceptions and racial backgrounds of people in the minority group but also the perceptions of them by majority groups.* We do not think this is desirable; groups should be able to define their existence for themselves. Our concern, however, is with outcomes and operational facts, not theory. If whites tend to include dark-skinned Asians in the same group with American blacks, then, for many of our purposes, dark-skinned Asians and American blacks are synonymous. They belong to the same group because they receive the same kind of discriminatory treatment.

Following is an in-depth discussion of the key points in understanding cultural and racial differences—Stage I.

1. *Cultural and racial differences exist, and they should be openly discussed and understood by all.* This is difficult for many whites to understand. Most of us were brought up to think of the United States as a great "melting pot" in which diverse backgrounds and lifestyles blend together to form a single "American" lifestyle. Of course, that is obviously a myth. While all Americans in the United States *do* form one huge culture, according to our definition, there are many identifiable cultural groups in the United States. In many ways we are a culturally pluralistic society, which means that a variety of different cultures coexist and make up our country. This is important to realize, for it is the negative consequences of being isolated as a member of a cultural-racial group that operationally define racism. If we refuse to recognize that there are different groups, or to understand them, we are likely to remain a society of racially determined haves and have-nots. More specifically, if whites don't understand that blacks are a different cultural-racial group, they are unlikely to be able to analyze and understand what they are doing to blacks.

Triandis (1972) presents a great deal of information relevant to cultural pluralism. His book develops procedures and variables which predict membership in various "subjective cultures" around the world, including many different groups in the United States. In classifying and analyzing subjective cultures, Triandis would look to such things as the frequency of a particular behavior, the methods of organizing thoughts in a group, and cross-cultural comparisons.

The saying "I treat everyone exactly alike" is heard often but is largely a defensive smokescreen, since none of us treats all people in the same way. We react differently to men, women, superiors, subordinates, teachers, students, strangers, co-workers, family, etc. And most of us do all this in the course of a routine day. For whites to pretend or to believe that they genuinely ignore differences when they deal with blacks is an error which prevents any kind of intelligent and meaningful interaction.

Blacks, however, tend to be more concerned with race than whites. That is, they are more concerned with what it means to be black in this society. Their daily lives are affected because of their race and their lifestyle, which is based partly on their African heritage and partly on the limitations and sanctions placed on them by whites. Blacks have been forced to take quick, sophisticated readings of white motives and intended actions. The consequences of doing or saying the "wrong thing" to a white have often been tragic.

Unfortunately, whites have not had to understand blacks in the same way in order to "get by" in society. Whites have merely had to meet the demands of their own culture. But understanding these differences is the key to bringing us closer together.

DiCesare, Sedlacek, and Brooks (1972) found that black university students who understood and expected racism were more likely to remain in school than those who were not prepared to deal with it. The study was done in Maryland, but the sample of students was socioeconomically diverse and contained males and females.

In related research, Gurin, Gurin, Lao, and Beattie (1969) and Sedlacek and Brooks (1976) found that blacks who believed they could "achieve" by their own efforts performed better in school than blacks who felt they were "up against" the system and couldn't do anything to help themselves. However, blacks who understood that the institutions of society control them in many ways but that it is possible to alter those institutions performed particularly well. The studies were based on secondary- and college-level black students.

This research raises an important point about the reinforcement or reward-punishment system for blacks and other minorities in the United States. Most whites, particularly white males, are accustomed to fairly clear-cut relationships between their actions and the reinforcements they receive: "If I work hard and get high grades in school, I will get a good job." But this is not always the situation for minorities or for women. Many blacks have been raised in an atmosphere of capricious or random reinforcement of their efforts or hard work. There has not always been an obvious link between their efforts and their rewards. Take the case of a black who may have been working hard to please a teacher by writing in the dialect and style of his or her cultural-racial group. The teacher, however had no understanding of what he or she was trying to say or how much ability the student had; so the student was consistently given poor grades. The next semester the student had another teacher, who was solicitous of blacks and gave them A's no matter what they did. If such unpredictable responses occur thousands and thousands of times, there will be no reason for a black to associate success or reward directly with his or her efforts. This occurs just as clearly with adults, who may be denied a job on the one hand but given welfare payments on the other. This random reinforcement system is especially insidious for black males. Black females, on the other hand, have traditionally been allowed greater access to education in the United States and in many ways have been more systematically reinforced than black males (Comer, 1972; Grier and Cobbs, 1968). Studies have consistently shown that it is much more difficult to predict the academic performance of black males than any other race-sex subgroup (Pfeifer and Sedlacek, 1971; Stanley and Porter, 1967).

Perceptions of sex roles seem to be critical in understanding the relationship between black and white cultures. Whites, for example, have developed a number of myths and stereotypes about the supposed extraordinary sexuality of blacks. Most of these myths center on the greater lust and passion that blacks supposedly have, as well as on their "superior" physical endowments. For whites, therefore, blacks have become fantasized sexual objects. At the same time there are corresponding fears—of everything from social sanctions to physical harm and disease.

Social sanctions may include various forms of exclusion from white society, such as unfriendliness by other whites and denial of basic societal rights such as job opportunities, mortgage loans, etc. There can also be fear of physical harm from irate whites or because of the supposed "physical" nature of black males. Fear of disease could involve anything from venereal disease to exotic ailments. It should be made clear that these are fantasies which do not require any basis in fact for their continued existence.

These feelings take different forms with white males and females. White males have been using their power throughout history to rape and seduce black females (Franklin, 1967). Comfortable or "polite" terms, such as "miscegenation," have been developed to describe the process, and there is an undercurrent of such activity and its related attitudes among white males today. White females, on the other hand, have been denied the freedom of movement and power enjoyed by white males; so their feelings toward blacks have taken on a more fantasized quality. Sedlacek and Brooks (1972a) found that white females tend to feel very negative about any physical or sexual contact with black males. Thus the myths and stereotypes appear to have made sexual contact a more anxious approach-avoidance conflict for white females than for white males.

The attribution of basically physical motives and characteristics, rather than intellectual abilities, to less powerful groups can also be viewed as a way of maintaining control over them. That is, as long as a group (e.g., blacks) is thought of as concerned with only physical issues, such as sex and athletics, it is easier to deny them jobs, homes, education, etc. In other words, if whites can think of blacks as animalistic, it is easier to rationalize negative behavior toward them. Since we have had a white, male-dominated society in the United States, control of black males seemed more important than controlling black females.

Blacks also have harbored sexual myths and stereotypes about whites that have been anxiety provoking, but for different reasons. The black male has tended to view the white female as the unapproachable goddess, the forbidden fruit, and so on. Being caught even *looking* at a white woman has often meant the physical or economic demise of many a black man—lynchings, rigged trials, or heavy social sanctions involving loss of employment. At the same time, the black man has at times been able to challenge the social power of the white man by using the sexual power attributed to him by whites. If a black man can seduce, or be seduced by, a white woman and get away with it, it is considered a victory over the white man. This has been historically true, and current manifestations of it abound even in today's far more permissive atmosphere. We know many black men who would give very serious consideration to the implications of being alone in a room with a white woman. But regardless of the black man's intentions or actions, he still contemplates the negative consequences that could befall him.

The black female, however, has perhaps been the most vulnerable of all. Historically, she has not been able to cry rape against the white man or call for the protection of black men. If the white slavemaster made sexual demands, the black woman was largely on her own—to submit, suffer physical or mental abuse, or try to find some way out of it. At the same time, she admired the power of the white man and the material benefits that could accrue to her if she pleased him. We can still see vestiges of these myths and stereotypes that were developed in early U.S. history.

Understanding the feelings and problems surrounding sexual relations among races is probably much more important than most of us have thought. Although the main points are covered above, several writers provide further information on this topic, including Allport (1958), Cleaver (1968), Grier and Cobbs (1968), and Hernton (1965).

The impact of sexual attitudes and behavior on the family structure of blacks has likewise been great. Indeed, the social structure of the black family has been very controversial in recent years. Moynihan (1965) has emphasized that the matriarchal nature of the black family has developed over such a long period that it will not dissolve with the elimination of racial discrimination. He views this as a negative condition and as a black problem, not necessarily brought on by blacks but one which must be solved by blacks. His thesis has led to a number of other articles and research studies aimed at clarifying the extent and nature of matriarchy among blacks, as well as its social implications.

A distinction between female-dominated and female-headed households is important for a better understanding of the issues. Households *headed* by females are more prevalent among blacks than among whites. However, when matriarchy is defined as female *domination,* it seems to be much more characteristic of white, professional families with non-working wives than of black females. Lower-class, intact black families appear to be even more patriarchal (male dominated) than their white counterparts (Jackson, 1973).

Other studies (Hartnagel, 1970; Nobers, 1968) indicate that black mothers without husbands are better able to cope with childrearing and to function as "parents" than white mothers in the same position. This pattern can perhaps be traced to the historical adjustments blacks have had to make.

However, it seems to indicate that the black family structure is not as negative or debilitating as Moynihan has described. The black family structure is a special condition or arrangement for a variety of social, cultural, and economic reasons. All that aside, it seems to be operating satisfactorily for many blacks. This lends emphasis to the cultural and racial differences in Stage I.

2. *Differences should be approached and presented positively in and out of the classroom.* The teacher or change agent who acquires knowledge of other cultures and uses it in a straightforward, positive manner is taking the first big step in the elimination of racism.

A study by Berger and Tedeschi (1968) found that among black and white boys, ages ten to thirteen, blacks were more cooperative among themselves than whites in the Prisoner's Dilemma game, which tests cooperation versus individual action in a situation involving rewards. If all players cooperate, they receive modest rewards; if they do not cooperate, they take a chance on receiving large rewards or nothing at all. Other work, by Lefcourt and Ladwig (1965) and Rothenberg (1968), tends to support this finding, which is probably related to a spirit of cooperation that develops among many minority groups. If a cultural-racial group is denied power by the larger society, a cooperative solidarity develops within the group. On the other hand, most whites in the United States come from a tradition of severe competition with others. Whites control our society, and young whites, particularly males, quickly acquire this trait. White children compete with one another, trying to win at whatever is involved.

The deeper historical roots of black and white cultures also tend to support these tendencies and traits. The African ancestors of blacks in the United States generally lived in less competitive, more socially oriented societies than the European forebears of most whites.

3. *Expressions of racial and cultural identity are necessary and healthy for cultural and racial minorities, and also for the rest of society.* Many blacks and other minorities are dealing with their cultural and racial identities within dimensions that do not exist for most whites. Certainly most people, white and minority, have problems of self-confidence and identity, but the minority person also has the pervasive racial or cultural "identity" issue to deal with. Each immigrant group started out at rock bottom of the social scale; they were considered inferior, were called names and made fun of. And of course they were given the lowest-level jobs. This was a culture shock and a negative but temporary phase.

First-generation children of white immigrants received much abuse in school and from their friends, and many felt there was something wrong in being Polish, Irish, Russian, Czech, and so forth. These first-generation offspring tended to deny their background and try to escape it. They changed their names, were ashamed of their parents, moved away when they had grown, and tried to be assimilated in the cultural mainstream.

The second-generation children, however, grew up without any negative associations with their cultural groups. Many wanted to know about their past and they searched for identification with their cultural heritage. They developed a pride, even a feeling of superiority, about their background.

Most third-generation children, however, are much more likely not to see any significance in their ancestors' culture, one way or the other. They can take it or leave it. This is because the majority society no longer practices negative behavior toward those groups. At this point we achieve a more tolerant society, where people are free to express their cultural or racial backgrounds when and if they choose.

The common use of the words "black" or "Afro-American" indicates that many young blacks are at the point where they feel more positive, even superior, about their cultural-racial group. The expression "Black is beautiful," popularized in the 1960s and 1970s, supports this conclusion.

People who refer to themselves as "Negroes" tend to be somewhat older and less anxious to identify strongly with their own race. When they were young, much greater emphasis was placed on white middle-class values and they were expected to emulate white culture. Straightening one's hair and "passing" for white were common forms of behavior. In other words, many "Negroes" remain at the stage analogous to that of the first-generation immigrant—denial and rejection of their cultural heritage.

People who refer to themselves as "colored" tend to be even older. Many grew up in a day analogous to that of middle-European immigrants, when being "colored" meant being at the bottom of the social structure. Unlike the case of middle-European immigrants, this negative phase lasted many generations for the "colored." Few people want to be called colored these days, but the word is undergoing revival among some younger people, particularly in international groups, as a word that once was negative but now can be proudly used.

Sizemore (1969) discusses a five-stage, power-inclusion process for excluded minority groups that has some similarities to the stages we discussed above. The first stage is *separatist,* during which an excluded group defines its identity. The second is a *nationalistic* stage, where cohesion centers around a common culture and the rejection of all other cultures. Next is the *capitalistic* stage, where earlier cohesion results in building an economic base. In the *pluralistic* stage, the group converts its economic power into political power. The final stage is the *egalitarian,* where the interests of any group have as much chance for expression as those of any other.

Of course, one obvious difference between most European immigrant groups and blacks is that blacks are more easily identifiable and thus are easy targets of racism. Obviously, blacks have lived many generations in America without progressing to a more equitable place in society. Some writers, notably Yette (1971), feel that blacks are in danger of never reaching a point where they can live and work in a nonracist society. Yette feels that since American society has become increasingly technological and machines do much of the manual labor, the original purpose for importing blacks is gone and the society may institutionalize itself toward the "oblivion" of blacks. That is, we may organize ourselves in a way that eliminates blacks. Because blacks are no longer needed, they will simply die out, much like the dinosaurs.

Thus, we support movements toward black identity and cultural and racial self-expression. Obviously, each event must be considered in context, but this is our general position. If blacks do not move through the phases for gaining power as quickly as possible, there is greater probability that Yette's thesis will hold. Also, keep in mind that we make this statement in 1976, and that, at some future date, support of black institutions could increase racism rather than allay it. For instance, if we were to reach a point where there is a power balance between blacks and whites and both groups are functioning compatibly, supporting black institutions might be worse for race relations in the country than denying support.

We are not concerned, however, with the argument that "if you give them too much power, they will turn on you, or maybe even take over." We are so far from any practical possibility of that occurring that it would be much better to spend our time on something else. This is not to say that blacks would be incapable of "taking over" if given a chance. Newly emerging groups have often been vindictive, particularly toward groups which have not yet fully emerged in a society—and this has been true of virtually every immigrant group. We mean that blacks have so little power in our society at present that such a takeover is not a real threat.

4. *Standard English is the white, middle-class dialect, but teachers and pupils should be allowed cultural expression through other dialects, even in the classroom.*   Considerable evidence indicates that there is a distinct black dialect in the United States and that its structural features and cultural uses are absorbed daily by young blacks (Baratz, 1973). In other words, blacks communicate with one another in a way that has its own rules and patterns. It is not "inferior" but it is *different* from standard English, and it is critical that whites, particularly white teachers, develop knowledge and under-standing of the dialects regularly used by blacks—or other minorities.

Aside from the specific details of dialect patterns, it is crucial that minority dialects not be viewed as inferior lan-guages without structure, rules of grammar, and communica-tion value. Moreover, it is an arbitrary judgment as to which dialect we call standard. A study by Williams, Whitehead, and Miller (1971) with Mexican Americans, whites, and blacks found that teachers tended to judge students' abilities on the basis of fluency in standard English. This tendency has caused serious misdiagnoses of intelligence and ability to learn many things, including standard English.

Obviously, it is not practical to teach several dialects in a typical classroom, but it is important that educators learn more about dialects and deal with them positively in their classes. Minority students can learn standard English along with an appreciation of their natural speech. Pointing out similarities and differences in the languages would benefit both white and minority students. If a teacher treats the use of minority dialects as undesirable, many minority students will be turned off and will not attempt to learn standard

English and probably other things as well. The scope of this book does not allow treatment of all the characteristics of black dialects, but the reader is referred to the comprehensive summaries by Johnson (1969) and Baratz (1973).

5. *Many students from cultural and racial minority groups have questionable environmental support for education and are not likely to be motivated by traditional methods.* Many black students do not have the typical family or societal "props" to fall back on that many whites have. For instance, a black student who is about to enter college may not have anyone in his or her immediate family or neighborhood who has been to college or understands the ins and outs that most educated whites take for granted. For instance, a new urban college that had been designed to serve blacks from lower socioeconomic levels suffered about a one-third drop in enrollment as the second semester of the first year was about to begin. Alarmed, the administration began contacting students and discovered that most of them intended to return but did not realize they had to register for each semester. A small point, perhaps, but events such as these can make routine problems seem insurmountable to someone from another culture.

As we noted earlier, white society does not have high expectations for minorities. White individuals and social structures are not geared to pushing black students toward an education, as is the case for whites. Because of the loosely defined relationship between individual effort and positive outcome, it may take very little to make a minority student drop out of school. If a white student drops out, there are generally pressures in the white culture that force him or her back into the system. The black, however, may drop out and never be heard of again.

The key to motivating any student is to reach him or her on levels that are important and meaningful to the student. The teacher who knows and understands the cultural-racial characteristics of students has a much better chance to motivate those students.

6. *Minority students may act differently from whites, and may generally react more negatively to authority in a society they feel has oppressed them.* Administrators, teachers, and personnel workers should not be surprised if hostility is directed toward them as representatives of authority. It should not be taken personally or misunderstood. Indeed, the most able minority students will probably be more resentful than average students because they understand racism and are trying to do something about it.

Allowing students to express their hostility but designing activities and programs to channel that hostility toward change can be a very effective way to work with such students. Don't cut off their hostility and negative enthusiasm; use it to motivate them. (Strategies for change will be discussed in Chapter 7.)

7. *Most white teachers are not prepared by background or experience to work with minority students.* This emphasizes the fact that good intentions and traditional academic training simply aren't enough.

Teachers must have specific information about methods of approaching minority youngsters. However, few curricula or training programs for teachers deal with such topics. Until they do, it is unlikely racism in the classroom will be eliminated. Even teachers from minority groups are not prepared to teach students from their own groups because of inadequate or incomplete training in college. That is, many minority teachers have had to learn methods and materials acceptable to the white establishment in order to graduate from a typical teacher education program.

8. *The characteristics associated with cultural-racial groups are dynamic rather than static.* Perhaps some readers would hope to find a list of words or "tips" on how to deal with

minority students in ten easy steps. But that doesn't work. Culture is always dynamic and changing. By the time this book is in print, some of the specifics we cite will no longer be true, but the principles on which the examples rest can be generalized and applied to new situations. They are not time-bound.

In implementing this stage we often rely on materials such as Noar (1972), the Black Intelligence Test of Cultural Homogeneity (the BITCH test),[1] or the Dove Counterbalance Intelligence Test (see below). The Foundation for Change[2] also provides material (for this and other stages) at little or no cost. All of these sources provide specific information but the Dove test, particularly, can help make the point about the dynamic nature of culture.

Items on the Dove test (or "Chitlin' " test, as it has been called) reflect a black, West Coast, middle-1960s ghetto culture. Most whites do not score well on it, but many blacks don't do well on it either. This may be because of geographical, social, and time differences: some of the terms have already come and gone; others may never have reached the East Coast; etc. It is therefore impossible to supply a list of words or customs that would be forever useful in understanding a given minority group. We can ask people, however, to learn the principles, keep their antennae out, and apply what they have learned to each new situation.

There is a type of test commonly used which attempts to measure the extent of an individual's cultural understanding about the society in which he or she lives. These tests are considered to be a measure of socialization and are frequently

1. Available from Robert Williams, Washington University, St. Louis, Mo.
2. Foundation for Change, 1814 Broadway, New York City 10023.

considered as important predictors of the work discipline of a prospective employee. You have all probably taken one of these tests. To demonstrate the cultural bias of these tests, several tests of alternative cultural understanding have been developed—one follows. Give it a try; the answers are on page 177.

THE DOVE COUNTERBALANCE GENERAL INTELLIGENCE TEST
A measure of cultural involvement in the poor folks' and soul cultures

1. T-Bone Walker got famous for playing what?
   (a) Trombone
   (b) Piano
   (c) "T-flute"
   (d) Guitar
   (e) "Hambone"

2. Who did Stagger Lee kill (in the famous blues legend)?
   (a) His mother
   (b) Frankie
   (c) Johnny
   (d) His girl friend
   (e) Billy

3. A "gas head" is a person who has a
   (a) Fast-moving car
   (b) Stable of "lace"
   (c) "Process"
   (d) Habit of stealing cars
   (e) Long jail record for arson

4. If a man is called a "blood," he is a
   (a) Fighter

(b) Mexican-American
(c) Negro
(d) Hungry hemophile
(e) Redman or Indian

5. If you throw dice and 7 is showing on the top, what is facing down?
   (a) Seven
   (b) Snake Eyes
   (c) Boxcars
   (d) Little Jobs
   (e) Eleven

6. Jazz pianist Ahmad Jamal took an Arabic name after becoming really famous. Previously he had some fame with what he called his "slave name." What was his previous name?
   (a) Willie Lee Jackson
   (b) LeRoi Jones
   (c) Wilber McDougal
   (d) Fritz Jones
   (e) Andy John

7. In "C. C. Rider," what does "C. C." stand for?
   (a) Civil service
   (b) Church council
   (c) Country circuit, preacher on old-time rambler
   (d) Country club
   (e) "Cheatin' Charlie" (the boxcar gunsel)

8. Cheap chitlins (not the kind you purchase at a frozen-food counter) will taste rubbery unless they are cooked long enough. How soon can you quit cooking them to eat and enjoy them?
   (a) 45 minutes

(b) 2 hours
(c) 24 hours
(d) 1 week (on a low flame)
(e) 1 hour

9. "Down home" (the South) today, for the average "Soul
Brother" who is picking cotton (in season) from sunup
until sundown, what is the average earning (take home)
for one full day?
(a) $.75
(b) $1.65
(c) $3.50
(d) $5
(e) $12

10. If a judge finds you guilty of "holding weed" (in California), what's the most he can give you?
(a) Indeterminate (life)
(b) A nickel
(c) A dime
(d) A year in County
(e) $500

11. "Bird" or "Yardbird" was the "jacket" that jazz lovers
from coast to coast hung on
(a) Lester Young
(b) Peggy Lee
(c) Benny Goodman
(d) Charlie Parker
(e) "Birdman of Alcatraz"

12. A hype is a person who
(a) Always says they feel sickly
(b) Has water on the brain
(c) Uses heroin

(d) Is always ripping and running
(e) Is always sick

13. Hattie Mae Johnson is on the County. She has four
children and her husband is now in jail for non-support
as he was unemployed and was not able to give her
money. Her welfare check is now $286 per month. Last
night she went out with the biggest player in town. If
she got pregnant, then nine months from now, how much
more will her welfare check be?
(a) $80
(b) $2
(c) $35
(d) $150
(e) $100

14. "Hully Gully" came from
(a) East Oakland
(b) Fillmore
(c) Watts
(d) Harlem
(e) Motor City

15. What is Willie Mae's last name?
(a) Schwartz
(b) Matsuda
(c) Gomez
(d) Turner
(e) O'Flaherty

16. The opposite of square is
(a) Round
(b) Up
(c) Down

(d) Hip
(e) Lame

17. Do the Beatles have soul?
    (a) Yes
    (b) No
    (c) Gee whiz or maybe

18. A "handkerchief head" is
    (a) A cool cat
    (b) A porter
    (c) An Uncle Tom
    (d) A hoddi
    (e) A preacher

19. What are the "Dixie Hummingbirds"?
    (a) A part of the KKK
    (b) A swamp disease
    (c) A modern Gospel group
    (d) A Mississippi Negro, para-military strike force
    (e) Deacons

20. "Jet" is
    (a) An "East Oakland" motorcycle club
    (b) One of the gangs in *West Side Story*
    (c) A news and Gospel magazine
    (d) A way of life for the very rich

Fill in the missing word or words that sound best.

21. "Tell it like it ...."
    (a) Thinks I am
    (b) Baby

    (c) Try
    (d) Is
    (e) Y'all

22. "You've got to get up early in the morning if you want to ...."
    (a) Catch the worms
    (b) Be healthy, wealthy and wise
    (c) Try to fool me
    (d) Fare well
    (e) Be the first one on the street

23. And Jesus said, "Walk together children ...."
    (a) Don't you get weary. There's a great camp meeting.
    (b) For we shall overcome
    (c) For the family that walks together talk together
    (d) By your patience you will win your souls (Luke 21–19)
    (e) Mind the things that are above, not the things that are on Earth (Col. 3:6)

24. "Money don't get everything it's true, ..."
    (a) But I don't have none, and I'm so blue
    (b) But what it don't get I can't use
    (c) So make do with what you've got
    (d) But I don't know that and neither do you *

25. "Bo-Diddley" is a ......
    (a) Game for children
    (b) Down-home cheap wine
    (c) Down-home singer
    (d) New dance
    (e) Meojoe call

26. Which word is the most out of place here?
   (a) Splib
   (b) Blood
   (c) Grey
   (d) Spook
   (e) Black

27. How much does a "short dog" cost?
   (a) $.15
   (b) $2
   (c) $.35
   (d) $.05
   (e) $.86 plus tax

28. A pimp is also a young man who lays around all day.
   (a) True
   (b) False

29. If a pimp is uptight with a woman who gets state aid, what does he mean when he talks about "mother's day"?
   (a) Second Sunday in May
   (b) Third Sunday in June
   (c) First of every month
   (d) None of these
   (e) First and fifteenth of every month

30. Many people say that "Juneteenth" (June 19th) should be made a legal holiday because this was the day when
   (a) The slaves were freed in the U.S.A.
   (b) The slaves were freed in Texas
   (c) The slaves were freed in Jamaica
   (d) The slaves were freed in California
   (e) Martin Luther King was born
   (f) Booker T. Washington died

Proper coverage of this first stage (cultural and racial differences) is important since it is a prerequisite to moving people through the other stages. If it is badly done, many people may be reluctant to proceed further. It has the advantage of being fairly academic and impersonal for white participants.

Many will approach it as if it were a class in medieval history; that is, with interest but with little thought of application. This is fine, since the more personal and the more applied material will come later. If understanding of the key points is achieved, participants should be interested enough to explore the next stage, which provides the evaluation for Stage I.

Also keep in mind that materials alone aren't enough for most teachers. Libraries, though well stocked with culturally relevant material, go unused by teachers without some training or orientation or principles around which to build curricula.

9. *Understanding cultural and racial differences, and designing appropriate educational experiences and reinforcement in that context, are crucial to any educational system.* This is really the consummate point in this chapter, and perhaps the most important one in the entire model.

3

How Racism Operates

Racism has been defined in many different ways, but some writers assume that everyone knows what racism is and therefore do not define it. Schwartz and Disch (1970), for instance, have compiled a book containing many interesting and well-discussed points but they neglected to define racism specifically. Similarly, Knowles and Prewitt (1969) approach a definition but never really state it. And the National Advisory Commission on Civil Disorders (1968) stated:

> Of the basic causes [for civil disorders], the most fundamental is the racial attitude and behavior of white Americans toward black Americans. Race prejudice has shaped our history decisively; it now threatens to affect our future. White racism is essentially responsible for the explosive mixture that has been accumulating in our cities. [P. 2]

Attitudes and actions are part of the commission's findings, but the definition is still vague, and it raises the term *prejudice*. Webster's *New Collegiate Dictionary* (1973) defines prejudice as an "irrational attitude of hostility directed against an individual, group or race or their supposed characteristics" and racism as "a belief that race is the primary determinant of human traits and capabilities and that social differences produce an inherent superiority of a particular race."

Hesburgh (in Glock and Siegelman, 1969) defined prejudice as "a detrimental or negative judgment on a person or a group rendered without sufficient evidence" (Foreword).

Allport (1958) defined prejudice as "an avertible or hostile attitude toward a person who belongs to a group simply because he belongs to that group, and is therefore presumed to have the objectionable quality ascribed to the group" (p. 8). The word "racism," however, does not appear in the index of Allport's comprehensive treatment of prejudice.

Daniels and Kitano (1970) define racism as "the belief that one or more races have innate superiority over other races" (p. 2). They distinguish between racism and ethnocentrism, which refers to the belief that one's own group is the best, superior to all others.

Ehrlich (1973) defines prejudice as "an attitude toward any group of people" (p. 8).

Thomas and Comer (1973) define racism as "the belief that race, or identifiable physical characteristics related thereto, is the primary determinant of human behavior and sets the limits for human accomplishment" (p. 166).

It appears that the definitions we have examined thus far consider *prejudice* as a rather general prejudgment process and *racism* as something more specific. The definitions also seem to emphasize attitudes, beliefs, and feelings. That is, they focus on what a person is thinking or perhaps doing. Thus racism and prejudice are analyzed and understood, and perhaps prevented, by concern over motives and thought processes. (What we have discussed thus far is the first major type of racism, *attitudinal* racism, whose nature and problems of measurement will be discussed in the next chapter.)

It is interesting that the word "prejudice" seems to be more generally used than the word "racism." Apparently, "prejudice" sounds less harsh and is easier to say than the more inflammatory term "racism." It is perhaps significant that Allport did not even mention the latter in a book considered to be the basic reference in the field. Because prejudice and discrimination have been raised more forthrightly and militantly in recent years, the cutting edge of the word "racism" has probably accounted for some social change, both good and bad. In any case, the shock effect of "racism" and "racist" can be beneficial if the terms are used effectively.

Many behavioral scientists distinguish between beliefs, attitudes, values, and feelings—among other terms (see Sheriff and Sheriff, 1967)—but these terms will be used interchangeably here. The purpose of this book is to define a process operationally, without worrying much about the semantics of the terms. Understanding the process is more important than the particular label.

Later in this chapter we will discuss racism in terms of outcomes rather than attitudes, which should demonstrate the utility of this approach.

A BRIEF HISTORY OF AMERICAN RACISM

Attitudinal racism has been with us as long as there have been human records, but the dominant form of racism throughout American history has been white racism, or the feeling that whites are superior to all other races and cultures. This feeling of Western superiority was not noticeable until the sixteenth and seventeenth centuries. When the New World was being explored and exploited by white Europeans, the latter rationalized and justified their inhuman and barbarous acts because they considered Indians wild savages, not really human. Other Western Europeans and their descendants also came to believe in their natural superiority.

Daniels and Kitano (1970), however, made the point that *The Travels of Marco Polo,* a book about the famous Italian merchant who visited China, was written in the thirteenth century from the perspective of a Western visitor from an uncivilized nation to a highly civilized one. Daniels and Kitano also noted that ideas of white superiority were so little developed in the early English colonization of America that after John Rolfe made the first American interracial marriage with Pocahontas in 1614, the couple was presented at the English court, something that would have been impossible a few years later.

Nonetheless, black slaves were brought to America, beginning in 1619. That they were a dark-skinned racial and cultural group very likely had much to do with why they were relegated to their lowly tasks. Schwartz and Disch (1970) report that negative connotations for the terms "dark" and "black" existed well before the sixteenth century. Before the close of the fifteenth century, in the mainstream of Western European culture, the word "black" connoted "soiled" and "dirty," and by 1536, "dark purposes," "malignant," and "deadly" were all associated with "black"—as were "foul," "iniquitous," "baneful," "disastrous," and "sinister" by the late 1500s. The devil was called the "Black Prince" and the "black arts" were forbidden pagan rituals in the sixteenth century. Also, people associated the night with danger (quite realistically), and thus the night was "black" in a special sense.

Many of the negative associations of "black" came directly from the imagery and symbolism of Christianity and the Bible. Blackness and sin, damnation, death, despair, ugliness, and evil saturate Biblical writing, and it appears that white American racism and American Christianity became interwoven and inseparable early in American history. The Western world's credo was synonymous with a Christian-missionary approach to the people of the new land, and the ultimate expressions of this philosophy were concepts such as "manifest destiny" and "white man's burden."

The goals of the early colonists were stated quite clearly:

> *Principal and Maine Ends* [of the Virginia colony] were first to preach and baptize unto *Christian Religion* and by propagation of the *Gospell,* to recover out of the arms of the *Divell,* a number of poore and miserable soules, wrapt up unto death, in almost invincible ignorance . . . and to add our myte to the Treasury of Heaven. [Quoted in Gossett, 1963, p. 18]

Smith (1967) felt that the Puritan ethic of hard work and progress was used to justify slavery and the savage treatment of native Americans because of the "manifest" cultural and "racial" superiority of the white immigrants. Thus the Puritan ethic was applied in different parts of the country to different minority people, based on local economic needs. Social Darwinism, a popular misconception about evolution that developed in the 1880s, postulated that the strongest and best cultures survive at the expense of weaker, inferior ones. This served further to justify many actions of Europeans and Americans.

While it is true that the great "robber baron" industrialists employed Social Darwinism as a primary rationalization, the fact that the keepers of America's collective conscience, the churches, also employed racist principles to justify their actions served to absolve the actions of all. Thus, in a sense, by wrapping racism in a cloak of morality, the churches, or

Christianity, became the driving force in the development of American racism. (The use of "morality" as a strategy to combat racism will be discussed in Chapter 7.) Many writers feel that the current racial and prejudice problems in the United States are linked to this development of Christian beliefs (see Glock and Siegelman, 1969, and Glock and Stark, 1966).

Additionally, the prejudice of one religious group toward another has been an integral part of American history. Since Protestants were the dominant religious group, Jews and Catholics received most of the religious attacks throughout our history.

It is not surprising, then, that American education—in a formal and informal sense—has been and continues to be racist. Historically, blacks and other minorities have virtually been ignored by our educational system. Segregation, poor facilities, poor teacher training, and the attempted imposition on minorities of education based on middle-class values have typified the past and continue to be true today. One has only to pick up a newspaper to read of racial disturbances and debates over desegregating schools and know that we have a long way to go in education.

Is RACISM LEARNED OR "INHERITED"?

Most behavioral scientists believe that racism is a learned behavior. As with all learning, it begins at an early age and is the product of interactions with influential persons, including family, relatives, friends, schools, and churches, as well as the mass media (see Clark, 1963). Some (Jensen, 1969, and Shockley, 1969) conclude that blacks are biologically inferior to whites, and, as their reasoning goes, it follows logically that if whites have come to think of themselves as superior to blacks, it is because whites in fact *are* superior! Their reasoning is circular and can be easily explained in terms of *learning* to be racist, regardless of any supposed biological basis for it.

It will be repeated over and over again in this book that all people, particularly white Americans, are socialized into being racists. Our goal, therefore, is to become better informed and to effect realistic changes in institutionalized racism. If all goes well, we can stop our children from routinely developing into racists as they grow up.

BEHAVIORAL RACISM

While the study of *attitudinal* racism has the advantage of focusing on individual motives, it also has serious limitations because it helps people avoid the *consequences* of their actions. By focusing on motives and thinking and feeling, people assume that if "my head is right" or if "I am well intended," everything will turn out well. Unfortunately this is not the case.

Most racism is unknowing or unintentional. Most people do not know enough about the sources or effects of their behavior to realize how it damages someone of another race. It is even more destructive as a collective action of the majority society. For instance, if a white belongs to an organization that excludes blacks, formally or informally, then he or she is lending support to a racist organization, whether or not he or she realizes it or has the best intentions. The *consequences* are that blacks can't get in.

"Behavioral" refers to a general area of psychology and related fields that emphasizes observable, measurable behavior as a focal point, rather than the motives and intentions supposedly within the mind and therefore not observable or measurable. If a person crosses a street and is run over by a car, we are concerned only with what we can observe directly; for example, walking, being hit by a car, physical symptoms, etc. We are not concerned with why that person was crossing the street or what the driver was thinking. This is necessarily a superficial treatment of the subject, but further information is available in Skinner (1971).

For the purposes of this book, racism will be defined as *the individual or collective actions of individuals in one group which result in negative outcomes for persons identified with another group.* The "other" group may be based on racial, cultural, sexual, or ideological considerations. This definition is similar to one developed by Downs (1970), but he restricted the groups to those based on color. Note that *results, not intentions,* are critical in our working definition. Because racism continues to have adverse effects, we are not especially concerned about the reasons why.

As an approach to understanding the process of racism, this definition has many advantages. First, it forces people to look outside themselves to see and appreciate what is happening to others. In that way they realize they may have unintentionally added fuel to racist fires and they may learn how to be more responsible in the future. The person or persons against whom racism is directed become more apparent. People who have never thought of the consequences of many of their actions should do so now. Thus the racist can alter his or her behavior and observe its effect on others.

This is not as easy as it sounds, but it is a practical first step. If we do not observe our actions in terms of their consequences, it is very difficult to achieve change because we have no standard against which to judge ourselves. Examining outcomes makes it much harder to use vague generalizations and excuses for inaction.

(It should be made clear at this point that many psychologists would quarrel with our use of "behavioral," by which we mean nothing more than the effects certain actions [behavior] create.)

Another important component of our definition of negative actions is the implied *power* behind them. The behavior of one person obviously embodies power and authority if it affects another person. Again, critics of our definition might say that it is so general it could include almost any minority group, such as left-handed pizza eaters and so forth. The acid test, however, is whether there are unfortunate consequences because some people are left-handed pizza eaters. If nothing unpleasant happens, there are no victims, even though the pizza eaters belong to an easily identifiable group.

A good "reverse" example might be the senior author of this book, whose name, Sedlacek, denotes his Slavic origin. However, nothing seriously negative has happened to him because of his Czechoslovak name. Of course, at other times in American history or in other current cultural settings, having such a name might well have had negative consequences.

INDIVIDUAL AND INSTITUTIONAL RACISM

An important distinction also must be made between the types of behavioral racism. *Individual* racism refers to action taken by one individual toward another because the latter is identified with a certain group. *Institutional* racism is the action taken by a social system or institution which results in negative outcomes for members of a certain group or groups. An institution or social system, which is defined as any procedure or set of procedures that is regularly undertaken to accomplish some implicit or explicit purpose, can vary from table manners to the manner in which agencies of the federal government are run. Most people tend to think of their behavior, particularly in race relations, as an individual, one-to-one proposition. Thus, if a white has not done something bad to a black recently, there is supposedly no racism; but institutions tend to dominate and control the lives of most people much more than they realize. Skinner (1971) feels that our behavior is dominated by social institutions and that, rather than spend our energies in search of individual "freedom," which is not really possible anyway, we ought to change our institutions in positive and humanitarian ways. Understanding that everyone participates directly and indirectly in institutions that practice racism is necessary to move us further along in the model.

One method of introducing the idea of racist institutional structures is through simulations, which include a wide variety of methods and techniques designed to portray some process realistically—in this case institutional racism. Thus Chapman (1974) used the Starpower simulation game[1] to introduce the topics of institutional racism and sexism to college students. Starpower, a bargaining and trading game, results in a three-tier society in which one group receives preferential treatment and is allowed to alter the rules of the game. Also using the Situational Attitude Scale (SAS; see p. 64), which measures the attitudes of whites toward blacks, and the Situational Attitude Scale—Women (SAS–W; see p. 166 and Herman and Sedlacek, 1973a), Chapman found that playing Starpower resulted in a significant change in racist and sexist attitudes, compared to a control group that played an unrelated game. Chapman also found that students were more interested in activities directed against racism and sexism after the game than before it. His study demonstrates the relationship between an understanding of racism and sexism (Stage II) and racial attitudes (Stage III). We will now examine and discuss the examples of racism in education raised in Chapter 1.

RACISM IN ELEMENTARY AND SECONDARY SCHOOLS

1. *Segregated systems keep blacks isolated in geographical pockets, which results in fewer facilities, fewer teachers, and less money spent per pupil.* We know of no school sys-

---

1. Available from Western Behavioral Science Institute, 1150 Silverado, La Jolla, Calif. 92037.

tem in the country that does not, directly or indirectly, practice racism in this manner. Minority students, on the average, receive a consistently inferior education by the common criteria that are used to evaluate schools. In cases where per pupil expenditure ratios approach equality, federal funds are often used to increase ratios for minority students. This money is called "soft money" in educational parlance and is often limited to highly specific purposes that do not necessarily coincide with student needs.

For instance, we know of a school district that had $100,000 available through a grant to spend on tape recorders but did not have enough money to buy adequate books for its students; the $100,000 could be spent only on tape recorders. Grants seldom provide general operating funds. Additionally, if a grant or project terminates, there is often no continuation or follow-up, as with other programs, and there is an overall patchwork effect. Many terminated programs may do more harm than good since they may trigger enthusiasm in a black student, only to curtail it abruptly and once more reinforce the unpredictable nature of white society.

For example, teaching machines and specialists in their use were provided a school via a grant. The students were enthusiastic about using them and began many interesting projects. However, when the grant period ran its course, no provision was made for providing funds for specialists or even for routine maintenance of the equipment. At last observation, the disabled machines were stored, unused, in the school basement. Here is a perfect example of institutional racism, which may be unintentional in many school districts.

That job discrimination and housing patterns allow blacks and other minorities to be isolated does not alter the outcome of our neighborhood school systems and funding patterns: minority students get inferior education because of them.

2. *Because supervisors are poorly prepared and perhaps*

are uncomfortable in dealing with teachers and problems in primarily black schools, they tend to make fewer visits to these schools. Supervisors, like master teachers, have a certain number of schools for which they are responsible. They provide general curricular assistance in elementary schools or expertise in particular subject areas at the secondary level. Regardless of their motivation, supervisors have been found to provide less time and assistance to schools with large minority student bodies. In one school district, supervisors spent at least 200 percent more time (on a proportional basis) with the white schools.

The outcome is that more time and money are spent on the schools that need them least. Typically, such indirect costs in favor of majority student schools are not considered in estimating the money spent per student, as discussed above.

3. *There are few minority people in supervisory or central staff positions in most schools.* Again, regardless of recruiting programs or promotion possibilities, there are commonly a small number and small relative percentage of minority personnel in high-level positions in many school systems. This has been the case in every primarily white school district where the authors have served as consultants. In an area where performance criteria are difficult to determine, it is easy for intentional and unintentional racism to flourish.

4. *Most elementary and secondary school curricula are oriented toward white middle-class children.* This seemingly simple statement is at the very heart of racism in American education. As educators, we have said: "Let's develop one system that is aimed at our biggest audience, the white middle-class child, and hope the rest can fit in somehow." This premise may seem administratively simple, but it has caused all sorts of problems.

For students who are not white or middle class, the schools seem at odds with their experience and therefore irrelevant. As this continues, year after year, schoolchildren who are not white or middle class grow more apathetic or hostile toward learning in general. The poor, the black—the minority students—are just out of luck.

Thus the results of our institutional norms are negative for minority children. But as educators, we are capable of doing a great deal more for these American citizens.

5. *Curriculum materials that are relevant to blacks and other minorities are now available but are little used.* This is a classic example of not focusing on the results of an innovative idea or program. The intermediate step of ordering and stocking the materials is not enough. They must be *used!* Procedures must be developed to ensure that *all* students, majority and minority, are reached with new instructional materials that aim at stimulating their interest in particular topics.

Minority students are typically not reached at all, while majority students are given a slanted view of society. The outcome is often negative for both the minorities and the majority: dropout and boredom for minority students and inadequate education for majority students.

6. *Schools allocate insufficient funds and personnel for work on race relations.* Despite the complex and far-reaching implications of racism, most school districts have demonstrated little if any real commitment to changing things. The establishment of Human Relations offices often becomes a convenient way to avoid the entire topic. Often given little or no budget or staff, these counselors are assigned impossible tasks, such as preventing racial conflicts in a large system. When, in turn, a school or system continues to have racial problems, the self-fulfilling prophecy is borne out. "We tried, but blacks can't even control their own," is a common lament.

In truth, it will take considerable resources and strong commitments of time and energy to eliminate the roots of racism in our schools, so well-entrenched as it is. One modest beginning is to identify the problem as racism, not as a general human relations problem or a communication problem, labels which make it easier to ignore the real issue. Indeed, not all problems in education are related to racism, but so many basic ones are that the situation demands a frontal attack.

RACISM IN HIGHER EDUCATION

I. *Biased admission standards result in fewer black students on the nation's campuses.*   Predicting minority student success in higher education has received a great deal of attention in the last several years. While most of the work in this area has been done at the undergraduate level, professional schools have also shown interest. The Association of American Medical Colleges is pursuing some of these findings to test their applicability to medical education (see D'Costa et al., 1974 and 1975) and the Law School Admissions Council has a minority program under way (Baird, 1974). It should be added that most of the work in college and university admission standards relates to black students. It is likely that the predictors identified apply to many other racial and cultural groups, but much additional research is needed. Additionally, regional differences should be taken into account.

Stanley (1971), in summarizing the work on predicting the success of what he called "disadvantaged" students, concluded that admission to selective colleges and universities should be based substantially on test scores and high school grades, irrespective of whether an applicant is from a minority racial, ethnic, or socioeconomic group. Stanley, who is pessimistic about the possibility of remediation for disadvantaged students, states that "an admissions officer ignores test scores at his institution's peril" (p. 642). While an increasing number of studies show that the same predictors (tests and grades) work about as well for blacks or whites (e.g., Farver, Sedlacek, and Brooks, 1975; Pfeifer and Sedlacek, 1971; Thomas and Stanley, 1969), there are also studies with contrary or unexplained findings.

For example, Clark and Plotkin (1964), in studying "alumni" classes of the National Scholarship Service and Fund for Negro Students, found that test scores were not clearly associated with college grades for blacks, and they recommended the use of motivational factors instead. Similarly, Green and Farquhar (1965) found that School and College Ability test scores correlated with the high school grades of white males but did not correlate for black males.

Cleary (1968) found that some tests overpredicted how well black students would perform in college—perhaps providing further evidence of the inappropriateness of the tests for blacks. Pfeifer and Sedlacek (1971) found that if standardized tests and high school grades are to be used to predict college grades, they must be assigned different weights because they do not predict grades for blacks and whites in the same way.

There are many reasons for a *reasonable doubt* about the efficacy of tests and high school or college grades in predicting performance in school. First, *there has never been an adequate study of the issue.* If we look closely at the literature, we see that nearly every study has repeated the same basic methodology: sample a group of minority students at one or more institutions, correlate their high school and college grades with Scholastic Aptitude Test (SAT) or American College Test (ACT) scores, and reach a conclusion. There are many problems in such procedure, some of which are obvious and some perhaps less obvious. For instance, the minority students who are attracted to higher education tend to be relatively homogeneous and unrepresentative of the larger number of minority students with the potential to do college work (Pfeifer and Sedlacek, 1970, 1974; Sedlacek, 1975).

A second and related problem is that there is evidence to suggest that the whole sociocultural process for a minority student attending college is different from that of a white. For example, a prospective minority student often has no people in his or her environment who are associated with higher education. Thus, he or she must decide whether to attend a primarily white institution and face racism and prejudice or a primarily black school that may not give as good preparation for succeeding in the majority society. Also, a minority student often requires a longer period to adjust to college than his or her white counterpart.

Most studies or tests predict only freshman college grades. Farver, Sedlacek, and Brooks (1975) and Horowitz, Sedlacek, and Brooks (1972a) provide interesting evidence of how the use of tests without consideration of this longer adjustment period can be racist. They found that if college grades beyond the freshman year are predicted for black students, different weights will be assigned to the high school grades and test scores that are used in admitting students.

Another point worth noting is that, in any dynamic system, it is particularly important to make predictions about the future and not to dwell on the past. There is evidence from the studies cited above, as well as others (Sedlacek and Brooks, 1970a; Sedlacek, Brooks, and Horowitz, 1972; Sedlacek, Brooks, and Mindus, 1973a; Sedlacek, Lewis, and Brooks, 1974; Sedlacek, Strader, and Brooks, 1975), that if society is to become serious about providing higher education for more minority students, it must tap great numbers of citizenry who heretofore have been untouched. The last few years have seen us help the "minority elite," or possibly those who had already adapted to the larger white society, for entry into our colleges and universities. There are probably many more minority students who need and indeed deserve higher education but whose culture, background, and lifestyle cannot be measured by traditional predictors, such as standardized tests, grades achieved in earlier education, or letters of recommendation.

There are certain useful nontraditional predictors of academic performance. The term "nontraditional" refers to a unique variable, or to a somewhat different use of a traditional predictor, but it is important that these nontraditional measures not be viewed as inferior or deficient. Minority applicants often come from a background which is culturally different and about which a typical admission committee knows relatively little. To use traditional predictors with such students would be to overlook the academic potential they have shown *in terms of their own culture.*

We do not advocate lower standards or second-class status for minority students; rather, we advocate the use of the most *appropriate,* albeit nontraditional, information in selecting such applicants.

The Cultural Study Center at the University of Maryland has begun a research program aimed at answering the broad question "Are there certain unique minority experiences which can be measured and translated into useful predictors?" Much of the research discussed here will be from studies in that program. The nontraditional variables we will discuss were developed from the interaction of such research findings with our practical experiences and those of others. These variables are sometimes called noncognitive.

Positive self-concept. Confidence, strong "self" feeling, strength of character, determination, independence. A strong self-concept seems important for minorities at all educational levels where it has been investigated. The minority student who feels confident of "making it" through school is more likely to survive and graduate. Although minority students have had to battle incredible obstacles and setbacks even to reach the point of applying to a college or professional school, they need even greater determination to continue. Determination is needed precisely because they come from a different cultural background than most of the students and faculty members they will encounter in school.

In addition to the usual school pressures, the minority student typically must handle cultural biases and learn to bridge his or her past culture and the prevailing one. DiCesare, Sedlacek, and Brooks (1972) found that blacks who stayed in college and adjusted to these obstacles were usually absolutely certain they would obtain their degree, in contrast to those who left school. Epps (1969) found that a strong self-concept was directly related to black high school students' success. Sedlacek and Brooks (1976) also found this to be true of minority students in special programs at the university level.

Pfeifer and Sedlacek (1970, 1974) noted that this determination may take a form whereby successful minority students appear considerably different from their white counterparts. They found that blacks who get high grades tend to have very *atypical* personality profiles *vis-à-vis* whites who get high grades—and according to norms based on white students. Thus on some measures the opposite use of the same predictor will select the best black and the best white students.

The successful minority student, however, is more likely to be inclined toward, and experienced in, "going against the grain," as well as being atypical. Conversely, blacks who look like typically successful white students on these personality measures will not do well academically. Thus there is good evidence that important cultural differences operate between blacks and whites in the manner in which the self-concept is operationalized.

Understands and deals with racism. A realist, based on personal experiences of racism. Committed to fighting to improve the existing system. Not submissive to existing wrongs, nor hateful of society, nor a "cop out." Able to handle a racist system. Asserts that the school has a role or duty to fight racism. As was discussed earlier, racism can take many forms. For example, an admission committee that has good intentions but uses inappropriate predictors to select minority students is committing an unconscious act of racism. This is racism because it results in negative outcomes for minority students, who are incorrectly selected, and it is institutional racism because it is the result of collective action.

Research has consistently shown that minority students who understand racism and are prepared to deal with it perform better academically and are more likely to adjust to a predominantly white school. DiCesare, Sedlacek, and Brooks (1972) found that black university students who understood and expected racism were more likely to remain in school than those who were not prepared to deal with it.

In related research by Gurin, Gurin, Lao, and Beattie (1969) and by Sedlacek and Brooks (1976), it was found that blacks who believed they could achieve by their own efforts (internal control) performed better in school than blacks who felt they were up against the system and couldn't do anything to help themselves. However, blacks who understood that the institutions of society control them in many ways but that it is possible to alter those institutions, performed particularly well.

These studies were based on secondary- and college-level black students.

Realistic self-appraisal. Recognizes and accepts any academic or background deficiencies and works hard at self-development. Recognizes need to broaden one's individuality. Realism in self-appraisal by minorities does not connote cultural or racial deficiency or inferiority. However, institutional racism results in inferior education and academic background deficiencies among many minorities. The minority applicant who recognizes this and is prepared to act upon it individually, or with the school's help, will make a better student. Again, the studies on internal-external control support this point (Gurin et al., 1969; Sedlacek and Brooks, 1976).

Additionally, DiCesare et al. (1972) found that blacks who have a more realistic view of themselves and society are more likely to remain in school.

Prefers long-range goals to short-term or immediate needs. Understands and is willing to accept deferred gratification. Since role models are unavailable and the reinforcement system has been relatively random for them, many minorities have difficulty understanding the relationship between current work and the ultimate practice of their professions. The earlier discussion about the "culture shock" faced by minority students supports the usefulness of this predictor.

In other words, since black students tend to face a greater culture shock than white students in adjusting to a white-oriented campus culture, we are not as sure about how blacks will perform at first as we are about whites. However, by the time of their sophomore year, blacks are about as predictable as whites.

The minority student who is not ready to accept delayed reinforcement, when combined with the other adjustments discussed here, will be in a great deal of trouble in college.

Availability of a strong support person. Has a person of strong influence who provides advice. In times of crisis the successful minority student tends to have a strong individual in his or her background to turn to. This individual may be in the immediate family, but is often a relative or a community worker. Many minority students do not have the "props" or support to fall back upon that whites typically have.

For instance, a black student who is about to enter college may not have members in his or her immediate family or neighborhood friends who have been to college or understand the ins and outs of the system, which most educated whites take for granted. As noted earlier, whites, individually and collectively through institutions, do not usually have high expectations of minorities and therefore are not geared to pushing a minority student to seek education.

Because of random reinforcement or the relationship between individual effort and positive outcome, it may take relatively little to make a minority student drop out or fail at school. If a white student drops out, there are generally many forces in white society to bring him or her back into the educational system. But the minority student may drop out and never be heard from again.

The minority stduent who has at least one strong support person in his or her background is more likely to get through the many and very difficult adjustments required of most minorities in a predominantly white school.

Successful leadership experience. Has shown ability to organize and influence others within his or her cultural-racial context. The key here is nontraditional evidence of leadership among minority students. Application forms and interviews are typically slanted in directions unlikely to yield much about the background of a minority student. The typical white applicant knows how to "play the game," and will have "taken up," and then be sure to list, a wide variety of offices held in traditional campus organizations. Many minority students will not have had the time or the inclination for such activities.

The most promising students, however, may have shown their leadership in less typical ways, such as working in their communities, or through their church, or even as a street-gang leader in high school. It is important to pursue the culturally relevant activities of the applicants rather than to treat them as if they come from a white middle-class environment. If the applicant succeeded in his or her culture and is now ready to "take on" college, this is evidence that the student has the potential to succeed.

Demonstrated community service. Has shown evidence of contributing to his or her community. This predictor is closely related to the leadership experiences discussed above, since many of the successful leadership activities of minorities may be performed in their own communities. However, community service goes beyond this in providing evidence of interest in and understanding of one's background and willingness to help and serve one's people. If minority students reject their background, it is likely they will have trouble in personal areas, such as self-concept, understanding racism, and realistic self-appraisal.

The standard application blank and admission interview typically do not explore different cultural backgrounds and tend to miss a great deal of data that are useful in selecting minority students. A school that is interested in optimizing its minority student selection procedures must have knowledge of the cultural background of a minority student and the implications of urban-rural differences, and must recognize that many minority applicants are not sure about what information might be of interest to the school.

Many problems of an ethical, sociological, and methodological nature must be considered in using such data. For instance, is it fair or reasonable to admit only the "superblack," who has all the qualities cited above?

Our feeling is that we must examine the question more thoroughly. In the long run, we must eliminate the sources of institutional racism which have created our current situation. Traditional predictors such as grades and standardized tests simply reflect the racism in our society. Until racism is eliminated, these predictors will continue to be biased against cultural and racial minorities.

Research on the difficulties of operationally defining bias has recently opened a whole new area for measurement and statistics specialists. A given test or predictor may be biased or unbiased, depending on the definition one employs (Cole, 1973; Hanson, Belcher, Sedlacek, and Thrush, 1973; Linn, 1973).

However, in the short run, admission committees must work with what they have. Minorities must be admitted in the fairest way possible. Unfortunately, unless a minority student has many of the aforementioned characteristics, he or she will experience great difficulties in most schools. This is bad for both the individual student and the school. However, as schools become more concerned with the social context of education, the cultural backgrounds of their students must be reflected in admission policies. For instance, the Association of American Medical Colleges (AAMC) recommended the seven variables cited above in the selection of medical students (D'Costa et al., 1974, 1975). The AAMC is also investigating other nontraditional measures.

II. *Faculty members have low expectations of minority student performance.* A number of studies have shown that the most critical variable in early education is the attitude of the teacher toward the student. If a teacher expects a student to perform well, the student does, and vice versa. Too often, too little is expected of the minority student, and the self-fulfilling prophecy becomes a reality (Silberman, 1964, 1970; Rosenthal and Jacobson, 1968). This problem exists at all levels of education. Even after minority students have gone as far as college, instructors are reluctant to believe that they are as able as their white counterparts (Christensen and Sedlacek, 1974).

Rubovits and Maehr (1973) found that the treatment

of students by teachers at the elementary level was influenced by the student's race. White students received more and better kinds of interaction with teachers, even when the teachers had been led to believe that both the black and the white students were "gifted." Thus the evidence is rather strong that teachers expect less of blacks; and teacher expectations are probably the most important determinant of educational achievement.

III. *Most student activities are organized primarily for whites.* In a university or college environment, a student is expected to choose a lifestyle from among those offered (directly or indirectly) by the school. On a primarily white campus, however, most of these activities are geared toward a white lifestyle. For instance, musical programs tend to emphasize the interests of whites, rather than blacks. Thus many blacks have difficulty adjusting to a white-oriented campus and drop out of school (DiCesare, Sedlacek, and Brooks, 1972). They feel much like Ralph Ellison's "invisible man" (1953). Everyone and everything is oriented in another direction. Minority students are left out. Again, the outcome for a minority student on such a campus is negative.

IV. *Most counselors are not knowledgeable about minority students' problems and concerns.* Counselor-training programs suffer from many of the same problems as teacher-training programs: little realistic orientation to minority issues and problems (Sedlacek, Brooks, and Herman, 1971). Burrell and Rayder (1971) found that white counselors were ineffective with blacks, and other studies (Barney and Hall, 1965; Green, 1966; Vontress, 1968) concluded that only with great understanding of the needs and backgrounds of blacks can whites be successful as counselors to blacks. Unfortunately, a great deal of work and training for both new and experienced counselors is needed before the situation is likely to change.

V. *There are only limited course offerings that are relevant to minority students.* This situation parallels the lack of curricular materials at lower levels of education. Minority studies programs have been growing around the country (Sedlacek, Lewis, and Brooks, 1974), but programs at most schools remain isolated in the curriculum, and have relatively little impact on black or white students. This includes both traditional courses, such as black history, and more vocationally oriented courses, such as counseling blacks. This has an overall negative effect on minority students.

VI. *Few minority personnel are in key decision-making roles.* More minority applicants are being hired as human relations experts, assistants to administrators, and so forth, but very few blacks have powerful roles at most colleges and universities. National teaching-faculty data are not available, but there are very few minority professors at most schools. Again, whatever the reasons, the outcomes are negative.

VII. *Programs for minority students tend to be understaffed and underfunded.* As in the lower levels of education, minority staff members are often hired on "soft money" or special grants and are given small resources for accomplishing large tasks. Such programs may do more harm than good since many have little chance of success as currently constituted. The minority staff member fails, and again the self-fulfilling prophecy is demonstrated.

VIII. *Schools commit little of their own funds to minority student programs.* The issue of "soft money" is again raised. Many schools take the expenditure of their regular budgeted funds far more seriously than federal grants for "educational frills."

IMPLEMENTATION OF STAGE II

The above were only a few examples of racism. The full implementation of Stage II requires that additional points, other than those raised thus far, be understood.

One of the major themes in American racism is that

since most of the society is run by and for whites, racism is primarily a white problem. And unless whites are willing to change individually and collectively, through their institutions, white racism is likely to remain.

Racism is analogous to alcoholism in that if we say "Well, maybe I drink a little too much occasionally, but I am *not* an alcoholic," we are not likely to begin to deal with our problem. However, if we understand and admit our problem, we can begin to work on it. We are all racists and we should begin to work on our problem.

While the concept of institutional racism may be difficult for many people to understand, there has been progress in getting educators, parents, and students to understand how school policy and the everyday practices of teachers, administrators, and policymakers could be detrimental to minorities, regardless of their good intentions.

Many people still operate at a comfortable intellectual level at this stage, but some will begin to grow defensive, perhaps in anticipation of what is to come.

Several points about the development of these procedures for eliminating racism should be reiterated here. The first stage, a demonstration of cultural and racial differences in our society, aimed at getting people to understand where they are and getting them involved. If they could see that differences can be approached positively and *then* can be made to see that it is the whites who must work on *their* problem, the whole structure of orientation and outlook will be easier to understand.

A shift in emphasis is also important. An attempt is made to shift people from the typical feeling that only blacks can solve their problems to feeling that all this is a white problem, individually and collectively.

4

Examining Racial Attitudes

Studying racial attitudes may seem to the reader to contradict the key point of our thesis, that is, emphasizing consequences rather than motives. We *do* deal with attitudes, but only as sources of behavior. And the only reason for discussing attitudes is that people must examine their feelings before they ultimately *do* something about racism. First, most people seem to feel that racial attitudes and racism are synonymous. Second, dealing with attitudes reinforces the individual responsibility that is so critical to generating change.

It is our intent to make people aware of their attitudes and how those attitudes may affect their behavior. Individuals must look at themselves in their relations with others to glimpse the complex emotional chain reaction represented by their racial attitudes.

DEVELOPMENT OF THE SITUATIONAL ATTITUDE SCALE (SAS)

We (Sedlacek, 1972; Sedlacek and Brooks, 1970b; and Sedlacek, Brooks, and Chaples, 1972) have summarized the problems of measuring racial attitudes: (1) with rapid societal change, attitudinal measures must be contemporary to be useful and item content must be updated; (2) evidence for the validity of measurement scales has been lacking; and (3) current measurement of whites' attitudes toward blacks is made more difficult because being tolerant or positive toward blacks is now "the thing to do." It now appears to be less socially acceptable to verbalize or admit, even to oneself, one's prejudices (Sedlacek and Brooks, 1970c, 1971a).

The Situational Attitude Scale (SAS) was developed to measure the attitudes of whites toward blacks by reducing the measurement problems mentioned above. To provide a racial context and make psychological withdrawal difficult, ten personal and social situations, with some relevance to a racial response, were created (see Exhibit 1).

EXHIBIT 1

INSTRUCTIONS AND SITUATIONS FROM THE SAS*
INSTRUCTIONS

This questionnaire measures how people think and feel about a number of social and personal incidents and situations. It is not a test so there are no right or wrong answers. The questionnaire is anonymous so please *do not sign your name.*

Each item or situation is followed by 10 descriptive word scales. Your task is to select, for each descriptive scale, the rating which best describes *your* feelings toward the item.

Sample item: Going out on a date

happy　| A | B | C | D | E |　sad

You would indicate the direction and extent of your feelings (e.g., you might select B) by indicating your choice (B) on your response sheet by blackening in the appropriate space for that word scale. *Do not mark on the booklet. Please respond to all word scales.*

Sometimes you may feel as though you had the same item before on the questionnaire. This will not be the case, so *do not look back and forth* through the items. Do not try to remember how you checked similar items earlier in the questionnaire. *Make each item a separate and independent judgment.* Respond as honestly as possible without puzzling over individual items. Respond with your first impressions whenever possible.

SITUATIONS

Form A

I. A new family moves in next door to you.

II. You read in the paper that a man has raped a woman.

III. It is evening and a man appears at your door saying he is selling magazines.

IV. You are walking down the street alone and must pass a corner where a group of five young men are loitering.

V. Your best friend has just become engaged.

VI. You are stopped for speeding by a policeman.

VII. A new person joins your social group.

VIII. You see a youngster steal something in a dimestore.

IX. Some students on campus stage a demonstration.

X. You get on a bus and you are the only person who has to stand.

Form B

I. A new black family moves in next door to you.

II. You read in the paper that a black man has raped a white woman.

III. It is evening and a black man appears at your door saying he is selling magazines.

IV. You are walking down the street alone and must pass a corner where a group of five young black men are loitering.

V. Your best friend has just become engaged to a black person.

VI. You are stopped for speeding by a black policeman.

VII. A new black person joins your social group.

VIII. You see a black youngster steal something in a dimestore.

IX. Some black students on campus stage a demonstration.

X. You get on a bus that has all black people aboard and you are the only person who has to stand.

*The Situational Attitude Scale is copyrighted and available from Natresources, Inc., 520 N. Michigan Ave., Chicago, Ill. 60611.

The situations represent instances where race might influence reactions to a given situation. Two forms of the SAS were developed. Each contains the same situations, scales, and instructions, except that the word "black" was inserted into each situation in form B. The "positive pole" for each item was varied randomly from right to left to avoid response set. By directly comparing responses to forms A and B, one can determine to what extent having a black in the situation influences the response of a white respondent. Detailed information on the SAS is provided in a manual (Sedlacek and Brooks, 1972b), and some of it is discussed below.

SCALE DESCRIPTIONS

The SAS yields ten situation scores which indicate the degree of positive attitudes held toward blacks. Each situation is self-descriptive, but the situations are relatively independent of one another and should be considered separately (Brooks and Sedlacek, 1972; Sedlacek and Brooks, 1970b, 1970d). Research indicates that situations I (new family next door) and V (best friend engaged) often generate the strongest negative reactions among white respondents. Situations III (magazine salesman) and VI (policeman) have consistently shown *more positive* attitudes by whites toward blacks than when race was not mentioned. In other words, whites seem to *prefer* blacks in situations III and VI.

The reasons for these findings are still being explored, although the best explanation seems to be that a magazine salesman and a policeman fulfill social service roles that are remote from intimate or personal interaction and that whites commonly view blacks as appropriately filling such roles in the society. Occupational information per se did not seem to be related to the race of the person in the situations (Brooks, 1971; Brooks and Sedlacek, 1972). For example, if we give a person the occupation of "doctor," the same pattern of differences between forms A and B (discussed above) emerges.

We demonstrated the importance of situations in providing the appropriate context for measuring racial attitudes by trying the SAS methodology with belief items that are not related to race and by finding no differences between the two forms (Sedlacek and Brooks, 1970e). The conclusion that is drawn from SAS situations is, "It's okay to have blacks sell me magazines or be policemen, but they had better not move next door or get engaged to any of my friends!"

USES OF THE SAS

The SAS can be used in a variety of ways and for such purposes as human relations training, program evaluation, research, and individual considerations. Wherever groups are interested in increasing their racial awareness or interracial sensitivity, giving the SAS questionnaire is appropriate (Sedlacek, 1972). A single administration of form B alone, followed by a group discussion of the results, is a convenient way for a group leader to raise the issue of racial attitudes. A skilled leader should be prepared to deal with the denial of negative attitudes, as well as criticism of the scale, by group members.

While the scale can be criticized for many reasons, the purpose of the discussion should be the results, not the attitude scale. Different attitudes evoked by the situations or items can be analyzed and discussed and the leader can build on these discussions and lead the group toward desired outcomes. Group results can also be discussed, in comparison to norms in the manual.

Forms A and B may be administered to a group and differences in mean (average) responses to each form can be compared and discussed. The preferred method of doing this is to randomly assign half the group form A and the other half form B. This has the advantage of providing a kind of instant norming on the group itself, so that the appropriateness of a particular norm or reference group from the manual need not be discussed. Again, a skilled group leader should be able to keep discussion focused on the differences and the reasons for them. We recommend that at least ten people complete each form so that a fairly stable mean estimate can be obtained. (Table 1 presents data from such a use of the SAS.) For smaller groups we recommend administration of form B only.

Table 1 shows that white university students and their parents had generally negative attitudes toward blacks. However, parents were more negative than students in their reactions toward a new black family's moving next door and a black youngster's stealing in a dimestore.

Program Evaluation Aside from using the SAS as a tool to promote group discussion, it can be used solely to evaluate the success or failure of a human relations or race relations training program. For instance, form B can be given to participants before and after a program, and any change in racial attitudes can be taken as an index of the success or failure of the program. Forms A *and* B can be given before and after a program, and the amount of mean difference afterward, compared to the first administration, can be determined and analyzed by both situation and item. However, it is best to compare the changes in response to those of a control group which is comparable to the program group but did not participate in the program. If the program group changed more or in different directions than the control group, the program evaluator is in a good position to attribute the change to the program itself. We also recommend that at least ten people be in any group that completes the SAS. Chapman (1974) demonstrated the use of the SAS as a criterion measure. He studied the effects of a simulation game aimed at increasing racial awareness and found that such a process could make a difference on the SAS scores.

TABLE 1

Means and Standard Deviations of SAS Situation Scores* for Parents (N = 78) and Students (N = 229) at the University of Maryland†

Situation‡	Form A: Parents		Form A: Students		Form B: Parents		Form B: Students	
	Mean	SD	Mean	SD	Mean	SD	Mean	SD
I. New family next door (F, FG)	2.98	0.51	2.76	0.52	2.59	0.65	2.64	0.75
II. Man raped woman (G)	1.09	0.39	1.48	0.47	0.98	0.37	1.38	0.50
III. Man selling magazines (F, G)	1.71	0.58	1.81	0.55	1.98	0.57	2.14	0.63
IV. Corner of loitering men	1.88	0.32	1.89	0.39	1.87	0.31	1.89	0.30
V. Friend becomes engaged (F)	3.14	0.63	3.09	0.54	2.47	0.79	2.58	0.82
VI. Stopped by policeman (F, G)	1.84	0.57	2.16	0.67	2.50	0.56	2.76	0.62
VII. Person joins social group	2.84	0.60	2.76	0.63	2.98	0.63	2.79	0.72
VIII. Youngster steals (F, G, FG)	2.58	0.46	1.90	0.57	2.30	0.44	1.86	0.50
IX. Campus demonstration (F)	1.93	0.56	1.99	0.76	1.73	0.62	1.86	0.69
X. Only person standing (G)	2.10	0.67	2.33	0.75	2.12	0.67	2.26	0.70

*4 = positive attitude; 0 = negative attitude.

†Reproduced from W. E. Sedlacek, G. C. Brooks, Jr., and L. A. Mindus, "Racial Attitudes of White University Students and Their Parents," *Journal of College Student Personnel*, 14 (1972): 517–520.

‡Letters in parentheses indicate analysis of variance terms significant beyond .05: F = form (A or B), G = group (parent or student), FG is the interaction.

Research   There are many research uses of the SAS. By manipulation of the racial referents in the SAS, any number of interesting studies are possible. For instance, we found that if the word "Negro" is substituted for "black" in form B, or the word "white" is used instead of omitting all mention of race, this did not affect the reaction of white subjects (Brooks and Sedlacek, 1970, 1971). Additionally, we found that Danish students tended to respond positively to form B but negatively to a form of the SAS referring to "Mediterranean foreign workers" (Chaples, Sedlacek, and Brooks, 1972, 1973). We found that Danes tend to respond to Mediterraneans in the same way American whites respond to blacks. However, Danes were very positive toward blacks because black are not a culturally relevant group in Denmark (Brooks, Sedlacek, and Chaples, 1972, 1974). It may be possible to extend the SAS idea to a variety of situations and groups and achieve experimental results with relatively little trouble. We are currently gathering data with the SAS in Japan and Australia to obtain information on how generalized the concept of prejudice is across different cultures.

The SAS has also been employed with campus police officers. Quite often the important role of nonacademic personnel in regards to race relations is forgotten. Leitner and Sedlacek (1974) found that those rated as successful campus police officers had more negative racial attitudes than those apparently performing less well. These results were used to help the campus police face the issue of what points were being emphasized in their operation.

We have also found the SAS to be related to other psychological characteristics. For example, Sedlacek and Brooks (1972c) studied the relationship between the SAS and the Dogmatism scale of Rokeach (1954) and the Authoritarian scale of Adorno et al. (1950) among 224 university students and found that negative racial attitudes were associated with high dogmatism and authoritarianism. We found the correlation to be strongest for SAS situations I (new black family next door), V (friend engaged to a black), VIII (black youngster stealing), and IX (black student demonstration).

Lewis and Sedlacek (1973) administered the SAS and a religious attitude questionnaire to 168 white university freshmen and found that those who were active in the church and believed in God and life after death tended to be tolerant of a black person's joining their social group and a black youngster's stealing, but were prejudiced toward a black man raping a white woman. Those with liberal attitudes toward abortion, marrying outside the faith, and pacifism were less prejudiced than those who held conservative positions on these issues.

Perhaps the most interesting conclusion from SAS research is that the same pattern of white attitudes toward blacks has been found in many different white groups. Aside from the groups we have discussed thus far, basically negative racial attitudes have been found in educators (Ball, 1971), residence hall staffs (Brooks, 1972), Midwestern university students (Eberly, 1972a and b), and older adults (Whaples, 1974).

Although we were concerned that the reading level required in the SAS would prohibit its use with less educated groups, we demonstrated that a version of the SAS employing simpler wording would yield the same results as the regular SAS (Rovner and Sedlacek, 1974).

With Individuals The SAS can be used in counseling or diagnostic work with individual clients or cases or as a self-evaluation technique. It is appropriate in any situation that requires general personality or attitude information. Obviously, in circumstances where racial attitudes are important, the SAS is particularly useful.

In individual cases it is recommended that only form B

be administered and that responses be compared to Table 1 on page 69, Table 2 on page 75, or one of the tables in the SAS manual (Sedlacek and Brooks, 1972b). If there is no appropriate norm, it is best to administer the SAS to a sample group in order to achieve some basis for comparison. This can also be accomplished by administration to individual clients over a period of time if no appropriate sample group is available. The SAS can also be given several times to the same individual to assess changes over time.

We found no appreciable difference in the results obtained from two independent groups and from a group that was given both forms in immediate sequence (Horowitz, Sedlacek, and Brooks, 1972b).

SAS ADMINISTRATION

In the initial administration of the SAS we were careful to ensure that our subjects had no knowledge of the different forms (i.e., A and B), and respondents who had questions were told to ask them in private at the front of the room, rather than from the floor, so that they would not "disturb others." The reason for this procedure, again, was to keep the subjects unaware of the differences in the forms. Trained white administrators were used to reduce cues that racial attitudes were being measured.

Several studies that were done after the original work seem to indicate that the SAS will yield similar results under a variety of conditions. For instance, the use of black administrators did not affect the results (Sedlacek and Brooks, 1971b, 1972d), nor did the use of "Negro" rather than "black" and "white" rather than the omission of racial referents (Brooks and Sedlacek, 1970, 1971). Nor did the insertion of occupational information in the SAS alter the pattern of prejudicial reactions among the respondents (Brooks, 1971;

Brooks and Sedlacek, 1972). We also found that, despite a strong social "set" among white college students to respond positively, they held generally negative attitudes toward blacks (Sedlacek and Brooks, 1970c, 1971a).

One encounters problems if the SAS is administered to mixed groups of blacks and whites, because the SAS is designed for measuring the attitudes of whites toward blacks and not the contrary. The measurement of blacks' attitudes toward whites requires different situations and items.

If the number of blacks in the group is relatively small, their response sheets can be identified as they are turned in and then be discreetly discarded or scored separately. Afterward, results can be discussed in terms of a comparison between white and black respondents and why the items and situations are inappropriate for blacks.

Since the SAS seems to be stable across different aspects of administration, it may be possible to administer one questionnaire to the blacks in the group (e.g., form A or a separate questionnaire) and any combination of forms A and B to the whites in the group—in the same way as to an all-white group.

Sex Differences on the SAS

We also demonstrated that there are systematic differences in male and female responses on the SAS (Sedlacek and Brooks, 1973a). We found that white females tend to respond more positively than white males to situations I (new family next door), V (friend becomes engaged), VI (stopped by policeman), VII (person joins social group), and VIII (youngster steals), regardless of the race of the person in these situations. However, white females tend to react negatively, compared to white males, to situations II (man rapes woman), III (man selling magazines), and IV (loitering men), regardless of the race of the person in the situations.

White females respond even more negatively to situation II (man rapes woman) if a black male is depicted as raping a white woman (form B).

Thus white female reactions to the SAS seem to separate into positive reactions to social or public situations but negative reactions to situations involving potential physical harm or sexual contact. (Chapter 2 contains a more complete discussion of the relationship of sex roles and race.) It is recommended that, wherever appropriate, the norms reported by sex be used (Table 2).

SUMMARY

The major purpose of the SAS is to raise the issue of racial attitudes, demonstrate that they can be measured, confront participants with minimum emotionality, and move on to the next stage, which involves learning more about our racial behavior from our racial attitudes.

The key points to be understood at this stage are: (1) Most people have negative attitudes toward other races and cultural groups. (2) Racial attitudes may directly influence behavior. (3) Racial attitudes can be measured and analyzed. The SAS was developed for that purpose. (4) Whites generally react more *negatively* to blacks than to whites, in a personal or social situation. (5) Whites react more *positively* to blacks than to whites in a service role. (6) The referents "Negro" and "black" evoke similar reactions from whites. (7) There is a strong social "set" among whites to appear to react favorably to blacks. (8) Whites' attitudes toward blacks must be measured in a racial context; otherwise, they can be successfully masked. (9) Racial attitudes, as measured by the SAS, have a direct relationship with dogmatic and authoritarian attitudes. (10) White females tend to react particularly negatively to sexual or physical contact with black males.

TABLE 2

Means,* Standard Deviations, and Results of Analyses of Variance for 1,114 White University of Maryland Students by Sex† on the SAS

Item No.	Situations‡ Bipolar Adjective Dimension	Male				Female				Differences Significant at .01 §
		Form A (N = 342)		Form B (N = 336)		Form A (N = 225)		Form B (N = 211)		
		M	SD	M	SD	M	SD	M	SD	
	I. New Family Next Door									
1	Good–bad	1.22	0.91	1.80	1.01	0.91	0.86	1.46	0.99	F, S
2	Safe–unsafe	1.13	0.91	1.37	1.06	0.85	0.88	0.94	0.97	F, S
3	Angry–not angry	3.35	1.00	2.94	1.19	3.69	0.81	3.33	1.06	F, S
4	Friendly–unfriendly	0.88	0.86	1.06	1.00	0.66	0.88	0.83	0.91	F, S
5	Sympathetic–not sympathetic	1.60	1.04	1.89	1.24	1.35	1.23	1.78	1.32	F
6	Nervous–calm	2.77	1.17	2.63	1.18	3.08	1.10	2.80	1.19	F, S
7	Happy–sad	1.43	0.83	1.91	0.97	1.14	0.87	1.54	1.03	F, S
8	Objectionable–acceptable	3.07	0.96	2.76	1.26	3.36	0.86	3.14	1.18	F, S
9	Desirable–undesirable	1.45	0.87	1.91	1.09	1.20	0.90	1.59	1.17	F, S
10	Suspicious–trusting	2.53	0.97	2.35	1.11	2.96	0.94	2.94	1.06	S
	II. Man Raped Woman									
11	Affection–disgust	3.39	0.83	3.50	0.80	3.70	0.63	3.64	0.67	S
12	Relish–repulsion	3.26	0.86	3.40	0.80	3.70	0.65	3.60	0.69	S, F x S
13	Happy–sad	3.26	0.85	3.53	0.77	3.72	0.64	3.67	0.63	F, S, F x S
14	Friendly–hostile	3.02	0.90	3.10	0.89	3.32	0.81	3.10	0.89	S, F x S

TABLE 2 (continued)

Item No.	Situations‡ Bipolar Adjective Dimension	Male Form A (N = 342) M	SD	Form B (N = 336) M	SD	Female Form A (N = 225) M	SD	Form B (N = 211) M	SD	Differences Significant at .01§
15	Uninvolved–involved	1.69	1.29	1.98	1.25	2.07	1.38	1.98	1.25	S
16	Hope–hopelessness	2.07	1.11	2.23	1.07	2.28	1.10	2.32	1.07	
17	Aloof–outraged	2.37	0.98	2.52	1.05	2.71	0.98	2.54	0.91	S, F x S
18	Injure–kill	1.53	1.11	1.55	1.19	1.33	1.21	1.28	1.11	S
19	Safe–fearful	1.78	1.20	2.12	1.12	2.83	1.11	2.65	1.03	F, S, F x S
20	Empathetic–can't understand	2.11	1.21	2.36	1.23	2.30	1.23	2.48	1.21	
III.	Man Selling Magazines									
21	Relaxed–startled	1.67	1.14	1.70	1.23	2.36	1.11	2.10	1.28	F, S
22	Receptive–cautious	2.72	1.07	2.32	1.31	3.26	0.91	2.64	1.23	F, S
23	Excited–unexcited	3.00	1.06	2.56	1.05	2.87	1.13	2.46	1.16	F
24	Glad–angered	2.38	0.69	2.09	0.64	2.34	0.61	2.09	0.59	F
25	Pleased–annoyed	2.78	0.86	2.45	0.88	2.81	0.80	2.49	0.84	F
26	Indifferent–suspicious	2.06	1.36	1.74	1.40	2.48	1.29	1.91	1.42	F, S
27	Tolerable–intolerable	1.67	1.08	1.23	1.13	1.75	1.05	1.24	1.12	F
28	Afraid–secure	2.64	0.99	2.42	1.07	1.69	1.04	1.93	1.18	S, F x S
29	Friend–enemy	1.96	0.74	1.65	0.85	2.13	0.74	1.61	0.81	F
30	Unprotected–protected	2.74	0.90	2.53	1.04	2.08	1.14	2.18	1.16	S

IV. Corner of Loitering Men

31	Relaxed–tensed	2.69	1.15	2.97	1.06	3.34	0.89	3.19	1.00	S, F x S
32	Pleased–angered	2.23	0.55	2.31	0.74	2.33	0.71	2.19	0.57	F x S
33	Superior–inferior	1.94	0.97	1.95	0.80	2.12	1.01	2.12	0.72	S
34	Smarter–dumber	1.31	0.79	1.47	0.76	1.54	0.83	1.72	0.60	F, S
35	Whiter–blacker	1.66	0.76	1.16	0.98	1.73	0.76	1.11	0.96	F
36	Aggressive–passive	2.33	1.12	2.62	0.99	2.79	1.01	2.76	0.98	F, S
37	Safe–unsafe	2.43	0.99	2.68	1.01	2.92	0.93	2.79	1.03	S, F x S
38	Friendly–unfriendly	2.07	0.97	1.82	1.06	2.60	0.96	2.28	0.97	F, S
39	Excited–unexcited	1.86	1.02	1.69	1.08	1.96	1.12	1.97	1.11	S
40	Trivial–important	1.70	1.02	1.97	1.16	1.86	1.21	1.85	1.04	

V. Friend Becomes Engaged

41	Aggressive–passive	1.88	1.22	2.28	1.27	1.27	1.14	2.37	1.13	F, S, F x S
42	Happy–sad	0.76	0.99	1.91	1.38	0.38	0.81	1.56	1.36	F, S
43	Tolerable–intolerable	0.64	0.87	1.32	1.33	0.30	0.65	0.86	1.15	F, S
44	Complimented–insulted	1.03	0.92	1.95	1.05	0.82	0.94	1.69	0.93	F, S
45	Angered–overjoyed	3.01	0.82	1.96	1.06	3.47	0.75	2.37	0.91	F
46	Secure–fearful	1.10	1.06	1.48	1.15	1.04	1.05	1.36	1.22	F, S
47	Hopeful–hopeless	0.80	0.90	1.52	1.29	0.47	0.76	1.03	1.22	F, S
48	Excited–unexcited	1.02	0.92	1.67	1.12	0.31	0.62	1.36	1.12	F, S, F x S
49	Right–wrong	1.08	0.99	1.90	1.38	0.75	0.98	1.37	1.29	F, S
50	Disgusting–pleasing	3.23	0.91	2.09	1.26	3.65	0.73	2.47	1.12	F, S

VI. Stopped by Policeman

51	Calm–nervous	2.87	1.25	2.30	1.52	3.37	1.02	2.55	1.60	F, S
52	Trusting–suspicious	2.00	1.22	1.12	1.10	1.88	1.28	0.75	0.98	F

TABLE 2 (continued)

Item No.	Situations‡ Bipolar Adjective Dimension	Male				Female				Differences Significant at .01 §
		Form A (N = 342)		Form B (N = 336)		Form A (N = 225)		Form B (N = 211)		
		M	SD	M	SD	M	SD	M	SD	
53	Afraid–safe	1.74	1.25	2.59	1.39	1.31	1.35	2.92	1.34	F, F x S
54	Friendly–unfriendly	1.30	1.14	0.94	1.09	1.40	1.18	0.88	1.05	F
55	Tolerant–intolerant	1.22	1.17	0.76	1.01	1.09	1.19	0.47	0.79	F, S
56	Bitter–pleasant	2.14	1.20	2.56	1.22	2.36	1.14	2.97	1.05	F, S
57	Cooperative–uncooperative	0.53	0.89	0.49	0.86	0.52	0.91	0.23	0.60	F
58	Acceptive–belligerent	0.94	1.04	0.75	0.98	0.95	1.05	0.45	0.72	F
59	Inferior–superior	1.88	0.90	1.85	0.74	1.55	1.00	1.76	0.70	S
60	Smarter–dumber	1.76	0.86	1.88	0.73	2.09	0.91	2.03	0.54	S
VII.	Person Joins Social Group									
61	Warm–cold	1.09	0.87	1.10	0.97	0.76	0.89	0.75	0.92	S
62	Sad–happy	2.78	0.78	2.57	0.96	3.14	0.87	3.00	1.01	F, S
63	Superior–inferior	1.64	0.65	1.84	0.52	1.70	0.67	1.95	0.36	F
64	Threatened–neutral	3.14	1.07	3.34	1.02	3.23	1.08	3.63	0.80	F, S
65	Pleased–displeased	1.19	0.84	1.45	1.05	0.79	0.79	1.00	1.03	F, S
66	Understanding–indifferent	1.15	0.97	1.26	1.26	0.80	0.94	0.83	1.10	S
67	Suspicious–trusting	2.56	0.94	2.79	1.06	2.96	0.91	3.23	0.90	F, S
68	Disappointed–elated	2.43	0.71	2.26	0.88	2.63	0.71	2.54	0.87	F, S

69	Favorable–unfavorable	1.17	0.86	0.76	0.84	0.81	1.01	S
70	Uncomfortable–comfortable	2.73	1.01	2.89	1.04	3.04	1.11	S

VIII. Youngster Steals

71	Surprising–not surprising	2.71	1.35	2.17	1.55	2.50	1.18	S
72	Sad–happy	1.04	0.89	0.64	0.88	0.54	0.79	F, S
73	Disinterested–interested	2.52	1.25	3.06	1.03	2.73	1.10	F, S
74	Close–distant	1.99	1.16	1.78	1.25	1.92	1.20	S
75	Understandable–baffling	1.52	1.24	1.70	1.23	1.34	1.10	F
76	Responsible–not responsible	2.36	1.25	2.11	1.25	2.17	1.30	S
77	Concerned–unconcerned	1.38	1.22	0.70	0.93	0.84	0.94	S
78	Sympathy–indifference	1.77	1.19	1.21	1.07	1.28	1.14	S
79	Expected–unexpected	1.83	1.10	2.06	1.17	1.88	1.01	S
80	Hopeful–hopeless	1.66	1.04	1.61	1.09	1.58	1.09	S

IX. Campus Demonstration

81	Bad–good	2.11	1.11	2.11	1.10	2.11	1.30	F
82	Understanding–indifferent	1.51	1.12	1.33	1.06	1.40	1.13	S
83	Suspicious–trusting	1.66	0.96	1.79	1.02	1.91	1.02	
84	Safe–unsafe	1.85	1.12	2.00	1.18	2.02	1.20	
85	Disturbed–undisturbed	1.87	1.18	1.62	1.25	1.51	1.24	
86	Justified–unjustified	1.75	0.93	1.66	0.95	1.44	1.01	
87	Tense–calm	2.02	1.18	1.73	1.13	1.71	1.08	S
88	Hate–love	2.12	0.78	2.11	0.66	2.12	0.74	S
89	Wrong–right	2.10	0.98	2.12	0.99	2.26	1.13	F
90	Humorous–serious	2.63	1.12	2.97	1.09	3.38	0.76	F, S

TABLE 2 (continued)

Item No.	Situations‡ Bipolar Adjective Dimension	Male Form A (N = 342) M	SD	Form B (N = 336) M	SD	Female Form A (N = 225) M	SD	Form B (N = 211) M	SD	Differences Significant at .01 §
X. Only Person Standing										
91	Fearful–secure	2.63	1.11	2.12	1.21	2.50	1.18	1.88	1.31	F
92	Tolerable–intolerable	1.04	1.11	1.11	1.09	1.04	1.15	1.02	1.07	
93	Hostile–indifferent	3.04	1.06	2.86	1.06	2.91	1.14	2.93	1.04	
94	Important–trivial	3.09	1.07	2.81	1.18	3.14	1.05	2.86	1.16	F
95	Conspicuous–inconspicuous	1.56	1.26	1.21	1.22	1.38	1.34	0.90	1.16	F, S
96	Calm–anxious	1.38	1.28	1.87	1.32	1.64	1.35	1.97	1.35	F
97	Indignant–understanding	2.88	1.08	2.65	1.05	2.86	1.13	2.77	0.95	F
98	Comfortable–uncomfortable	2.24	1.31	2.40	1.29	2.56	1.31	2.60	1.28	S
99	Hate–love	2.10	0.69	2.07	0.74	2.13	0.74	2.22	0.68	
100	Not resentful–resentful	1.04	1.16	1.10	1.11	1.15	1.24	0.94	1.08	

*Scale A to E (numerical equivalent, 0 to 4).

†Subjects represent a broad range of samples gathered between 1969 and 1971.

‡See Exhibit 1, p. 64, for complete situation.

§Results of 2-way analysis of variance (fixed effects) with F (form A or B) and S (Sex, male or female) as main effects and F x S as the interaction. Complete anova tables are available from the Cultural Study Center, University of Maryland, College Park, Maryland 20742.

5

Sources Of
Racial Attitudes

Stage IV, the sources of racial attitudes, is often a short phase, and often merges with Stage III, examining racial attitudes. However, Stage IV affords an opportunity to assess the intellectual implications of racial attitudes: how they develop, how they are perpetuated, and what can be done about them. Generally, Stage IV is less personal than Stage III, or at least it is taken less personally by participants.

We noted earlier that establishing early rapport with group participants is critical. It is equally important to build on this and improve rapport as one works through the various stages of the model. Stage III may work against rapport but Stage IV affords an opportunity to rebuild it. One should keep in mind that many applications of the model are possible, involving work with individuals, or community work, or effecting institutional change from the outside by using pressure groups or indirect methods. In many of these cases rapport may scarcely be present. If, however, rapport is defined broadly as commanding respect so that others are moved or influenced by your actions, it can be included under this general topic.

Role playing has been used in a variety of settings, for many different purposes, but it can be especially effective in forcing persons to examine the sources of their racial attitudes. King and Janis (1956) and Culbertson (1957), among others, have shown the advantages of role playing in attempting to change such attitudes. The purpose of role playing, as we employ it, is to generate realistic problem situations that call for action and allow the participants to act out solutions. This process provides the dramatic realization that one's attitudes often intrude upon and influence one's actions. Such experiences have much greater impact on the role player and other participants than anything a consultant says because their attitudes are perceived in a realistic context. Thus the point that the sources of racial attitudes are also situational is developed in role playing.

In the particular method of role playing that we have found most useful, one creates a situation that has relevance in an educational setting and is likely to involve racial variables—for example, settling a dispute between roommates who are black and white.

Second, three to six clear and rather stereotyped roles are created, such as a resident assistant, a black student, and a white student. The differences between the roles should be sharply drawn so as to encourage pointed interaction. (Poorly defined roles often generate vague or weak outcomes.)

Third, relatively little definition of the roles, other than their overstated stereotypes, should be given. This forces the role players to rely or draw upon their knowledge and attitudes in playing the roles.

Fourth, each role player knows only his or her own role and must deduce the roles of the others as the situation develops. Again, this forces one to use his or her resources in relating to others. Similarly, the observers (or audience) should be told nothing about any of the roles. Fifth, the observers or audience are given the task of observing, taking notes, and the like.

The recommended procedure operates as follows. The participants or role players are chosen after everyone has been given the general information that if they are assigned roles, they are to act solely on the information provided. They are told to continue acting and not to stop until told to do so—after fifteen or thirty minutes.

It is generally useful and instructive to assign "reverse" roles. For instance, it may be good to have a conservative, nonverbal participant play a verbal militant, a black to play a white, a male to play a female, etc. This accomplishes a number of purposes. First, it is a rare opportunity for the role player to learn what it is like to be in someone else's shoes. Second, it forces everyone to deal with the content expressed by the role players rather than with physical characteristics or past impressions. (This strategy is especially valuable and useful in later stages of the model.) Third, because people are playing unaccustomed roles, their many mistakes and misperceptions are quite useful in subsequent analysis.

When the role players are selected, they are given slips of paper on which their roles are broadly outlined. They are then asked to read these roles to themselves, after which they position themselves in the center of the group of observers and begin acting out the situation. One of the slips of paper should indicate that a particular person initiates the discussion. After the role players "warm up" and get into their roles, the consultants should observe them carefully and take notes on all points that relate to racism. Later, after one of the consultants calls a halt, reactions from the observers are solicited.

Care should be taken to avoid "having fun" with the procedure without learning anything. But if it is done well, role playing is both fun and instructive.

After we hear from the observers, it is often fruitful to explore what each role player thought was occurring in the situation before they enacted their roles.

A series of role-playing situations can be covered either consecutively or intermittently, but it is usually important to get the first one off to a good start by picking several people who you expect will be good role players and giving them sufficient time. Usually the group picks up the idea quickly, and future situations run smoothly.

Occasionally players will have great difficulty with a role. For example, a black female who was playing a conservative white principal could not bring herself to say "colored" or speak against hiring a black teacher—which turned up the fact that she had once been denied a teaching job because she was "colored." This provided dramatic emphasis to what the participants had learned, including the role player. However, a fairly well educated group of parents and teachers is able to get quickly into the spirit of the role playing.

At this point we would like to analyze a role-playing situation that has worked well for us and discuss its rationale and expected outcomes. The situation is a high school curriculum-committee meeting that is held to discuss the feasibility of adding a black studies course.

SUGGESTED ROLES

Role A: You are a high school teacher and a member of your school's Curriculum Committee. During a meeting of this committee you try to persuade the other members that a black studies course is desperately needed at your school.

Role B: You are a parent, serving on your high school's Curriculum Committee. You are against any "new fangled" curriculum changes that interfere with the three *R*'s. You argue your position strongly.

Role C: You are a local businessman, serving on the high school's Curriculum Committee. You really know nothing about education and are primarily concerned with costs and keeping liberals, radicals, and Communists from taking over the school. You are very vocal in your opinions.

Role D: You are a high school principal and the chairperson of your school's Curriculum Committee. You are concerned with keeping your job and dealing with pressure from the community, but most of all, you don't want to "rock the boat." Also on this committee are a student, a teacher, a parent, and a local businessman. You will argue for whatever the majority seem to want. As chairperson, you begin the action by asking for new business.

Role E: You are a high school senior and a member of your school's Curriculum Committee. You are the popular class president, get good grades, and are mainly concerned with making a good impression. You feel your school is fine just the way it is.

The curriculum-committee simulation usually generates a number of useful and important points.

First, it demonstrates, through role A, that one is often alone and faces many counterarguments and forces when one acts as a change agent. Being goal directed but still being able to handle diverse opposition is an important quality, which will be discussed more in the next two chapters.

Second, the role playing emphasizes the behavioral-outcome definition of racism employed in this book. That is, many of the types of opposition are not apparently race related or race motivated. For instance, having interest only in the three *R*'s may not be motivated by race, but the effect of this position is racist because it would prevent black and white students from knowing more about black culture.

Third, the situation demonstrates that opposition may be passive as well as active, as the role of the principal is that of a passive racist. He or she may not intend it, but the outcome of the principal's position will be racist, since it will work against a black studies course.

Another interesting point in this situation is the role of the student, who plays a self-serving role, opposed to change. This demonstrates that students are not always the allies of change. Indeed the formal student leadership in a school may lose a great deal if change takes place. Thus it may well be that a change agent would have to look to other than formal student leaders for supporting antiracist actions.

The Appendix contains a transcript of an audiotaped session in which the situation was acted out. Additional situations that have worked well for us are given below.

SUGGESTED ROLE-PLAYING SITUATIONS

Situation 1: Student-Teacher Conference

Role A: You are a sixth grade teacher. Two of your students, who are very close friends, are not doing well in school and you have brought them to your office to discuss their poor grades. One is black and one is white. You begin the session.

Role B: You are a white, sixth grade student talking with your teacher about your poor grades. Your best friend, who is with you, is in the same boat. You are below average in intelligence and act it. You try your best, but just can't do sixth grade work

Role C: You are a black, sixth grade student talking with your teacher about your poor grades. Your best friend, who is with you, is in the same boat. You are above average in intelligence and act it. You dislike school and don't study because the material does not interest you.

Situation 2: A Course on Racism

Role A: You are a teacher who is taking a course in racism. You really don't think such courses are of much value and are taking this course just for credit. You try to talk another teacher out of taking it next semester. After about five minutes, you suddenly switch your position and argue that it really is a good course.

Role B: You are a teacher who is excited about the course on racism you plan to take next semester. You are discussing the course with another teacher who is currently taking it. After about five minutes, you change your mind and decide not to take the course after all, and you discuss the reasons why you think these kinds of courses are of little value.

Situation 3: Black Teacher Candidate

Role A: Your school has a number of fifth grade teacher candidates. They are all white but one, who is black and is not as well qualified as the others. You argue with some of your fellow teachers that the black

should be hired, even though his or her qualifications are not as good, because your school needs a
black teacher.

Role B: Your school has a number of fifth grade teacher
candidates. They are all white but one, who is black
and is not as well qualified as the others. You very
much resent that blacks are given jobs in preference
to whites, especially when they aren't as well qualified. However, you would be against hiring a black,
no matter what. You initiate the discussion with
two of your fellow teachers.

Role C: Your school has a number of fifth grade teacher
candidates. They are all white but one, who is black
and is not as well qualified as the others. You feel
that the best-qualified teacher should be hired,
white or black, and express this view to two of your
fellow teachers.

Situation 4: Race Relations Conference

Role A: You have just come back from a three-day conference on race relations. You feel there is racism in
you and at your school. You are eager to start working against racism by talking to your colleagues
about the conference, what you learned, and what
you can do about racism together. You start the
conversation.

Role B: You heard that a colleague has been to a race relations conference. You have an open mind and
would like to hear what he learned, and perhaps
make use of it yourself. Let him try to convince
you, though, and make up your own mind.

Role C: You heard that a colleague has been to a race relations conference. You feel that race relations are

radical garbage with no basis in fact. You strongly disagree with any proposed changes or ideas which would in any way alter the way things are done now.

Situation 5: Student-Parent Group—Principal Confrontation

Role A: You are a high school principal and meeting with a group of parents and students is next on your schedule. You are running late and must attend another meeting shortly. You try to get rid of the group as quickly as you can. Invite the group into your office.

Role B: You are the black mother of a male student who has been made to feel inferior by teachers and students alike. There are no courses or activities that are relevant to your son. You know the principal has been avoiding your group and you feel he is a racist. Use whatever methods of persuasion you like, but don't be afraid to really let him "have it" if he stalls. You enter the principal's office with a group.

Role C: You, an irate white parent, are concerned that racism exists in the school, individually and institutionally. You are particularly concerned that your child is neither being exposed to his or her prejudices nor learning about other races or cultures. As you enter his office with a group, suggest specific reforms to the principal, and do not leave until you get answers to all your points.

Role D: You are one of only a few black students in your school. You have been treated badly, and also have been shunned by the whites in the school. You are lonely and confused, but you have been asked by your black classmates to attend a meeting a group is having with the principal. Say how you feel.

Role E: You are a white student and dislike almost everything about your school. You are part of a group
that is meeting with the principal. You are highly
intelligent and articulate and you sincerely want to
get the principal to change things. Work hard to
convince the principal.

Situation 6: Teacher Education Student Group in a University

Role A: You, the chairperson of the Early Childhood and
Elementary Education student group, are going to
discuss inadequacies in your school's curriculum.
Your role is to keep the discussion going and seek
a consensus. Begin the meeting.

Role B: You are a white student who is attending a meeting
of the Early Childhood and Elementary Education
student group. You feel very strongly that your
curriculum has been most inadequate in preparing
you to teach blacks. You argue strongly for curricular changes in this area.

Role C: You are a white student who is attending a meeting
of the Early Childhood and Elementary Education
student group. You think the curriculum is wonder-
ful and would not change anything in it. Argue your
position.

Role D: You are a white student who is attending a meeting
of the Early Childhood and Elementary Education
student group. You plan to work in an all-white
school. You dislike blacks and feel strongly that
there should not be any special courses on teaching
them in the curriculum. Strongly argue your
position.

Role E: You are a white student who is attending a meeting

of the Early Childhood and Elementary Education student group. You feel that all people are basically alike and consider yourself a true humanitarian. You are against any special courses on teaching blacks or any other group. Teaching is teaching, and you need no special approach or technique. Argue against any change in the curriculum.

Situation 7: Human Relations Officer

Role A: You are attending a meeting that has been called to deal with hiring a human relations officer for the district schools. You are strongly in favor of this and argue your position.

Role B: You are attending a meeting that has been called to deal with hiring a human relations officer for the district schools. You are a school board member and are against any change whatever in the school system. Argue your position.

Role C: You are attending a meeting that has been called to deal with hiring a human relations officer for the district schools. You are a teacher and believe that any increase in personnel should be new teachers, rather than anything else. Argue your position.

Role D: You are attending a meeting that has been called to deal with hiring a human relations officer for the district schools. You are a conservative businessman in the community. You feel there are no racial or human relations problems in the schools and that requests for human relations personnel are Communist inspired. Argue your position.

Role E: You are attending a meeting that has been called to deal with hiring a human relations officer for the district schools. You are a parent who is primarily concerned with increased school costs. You argue strongly against anything that costs more money.

Role F: You are attending a meeting that has been called to deal with hiring a human relations officer for the district schools. You are the superintendent of schools, and you wish to hold on to your job and avoid controversy. You simply reflect the consensus in the group. Start the meeting.

RACIAL STEREOTYPES

1. *We all hold racial stereotypes that determine how we feel and act toward other races.* The SAS has demonstrated this point, which establishes a causal link between attitudes and behavior. Other evidence, however, is very mixed on whether there is a cause-effect relationship between attitudes and behavior.

Tittle and Hill (1967) observe that as the measurement of attitudes improves, so will the likelihood of improved prediction of overt behavior. The SAS, as we discussed earlier, should provide better measurement than older racial attitude scales. Additionally, a number of writers have provided evidence of a link between attitudes and behavior (e.g., DeFleur and Wester, 1958; Fendrich, 1965, 1967; Hyman, 1949; Warner and DeFleur, 1969; and Weissburg, 1965).

One investigator who has reviewed extensive research in changing racial attitudes is Amir (1969), who studied a number of research articles on the effects of intergroup contact on ethnic relations. The investigations included both intra- and cross-cultural studies of contact between various ethnic groups. Amir observed that increasing evidence in the literature supports the view that contact between members of ethnic groups tends to produce changes in attitudes between these groups. However, the direction of the changes depends largely on the conditions under which contact has taken place. "Favorable" conditions tend to reduce prejudice, but "unfavorable" conditions may increase intergroup tension and prejudice.

Some of the favorable conditions which tend to reduce prejudice are: (a) equal-status contact between the members of the various ethnic groups, (b) contact between members of a majority group and higher-status members of a minority group, (c) "authority" and/or the social climate that favors and promotes intergroup contact, (d) contact of an intimate rather than a casual nature, (e) ethnic intergroup contact that is pleasant or rewarding, and (f) interaction of members of both groups in important group activities or development of common or superordinate goals that are higher ranking in importance than the individual goals of each group.

In a study of 1,391 college students we found that the more friends of another race blacks had, the more comfortable they felt with someone of another race, and the less they felt that whites are racist, the more likely they would be to marry someone of another race and the less they felt their own mothers were bigoted (Brooks, Sedlacek, and Mindus, 1973).

In a related study, we found that black and white students at a predominantly white university felt most comfortable in an integrated situation (50 percent black, 50 percent white), less comfortable when either was in the majority, and least comfortable when either was in the minority. Exceptions —where students preferred to be in the majority—involved a party, a blind date, and major surgery. Whites generally felt more comfortable than blacks in most situations. Blacks felt more comfortable than whites in an integrated neighborhood or dormitory situation. We concluded that, despite some problems, the results indicated that blacks and whites are approaching equality in their relations with one another (Merritt, Sedlacek, and Brooks, 1974).

We suggest, therefore, that the relationship between racial attitudes and behavior is more complicated and indirect than was previously thought. We also suggest that knowledge of one's racial attitudes is an important prerequisite to action, but that knowledge is *only one* prerequisite. Without knowledge of racial and cultural differences, the process of racism, the nature of goals and how to set them, and strategies for accomplishing those goals, a change in behavior is unlikely—regardless of a person's knowledge of his or her racial attitudes. Our model for changing racist behavior provides a series of vital interlocking steps that ultimately link up attitudes and behavior.

A good analogy might be teaching someone how an engine and an automobile work. Unless that person understands the relationship between the engine and the other parts of a car (its wheels, gears, brakes, etc.), what gasoline does, where he or she might want to go in a car, and how to drive it, the principles of engine design remain interesting but abstract, and that person remains immobile.

2. *Textbooks help perpetuate racial stereotypes.*   While progress has been made by means of new textbooks, there are still many problems in how minorities are depicted (Banks, 1969; Glock and Siegelman, 1969; Silberman, 1970). Many changes are simply a token or cosmetic overhaul of a "classic" text. For instance, simply "shading" Dick and Jane to make them appear black will not affect the basic values and lifestyle depicted in the suburb-oriented readers. More books that are well written and that also show minorities in their own context are available, but many teachers do not use them adequately, if at all.

Teachers fail to employ the available materials for a variety of reasons, including a lack of understanding of a new book, being comfortable with the old book, fear of failure, potential embarrassment, and their opposition to specific or general points raised or depicted in the new books.

3. *The nature of prejudice and racism should be taught at all educational levels.* Again, a source or reason for our racial attitudes is that they develop without our dealing with them directly in our schools. Without this exposure and discussion, we know how they will develop. This is particularly crucial for young whites in that, without help, they are not likely to be able to avoid becoming racists.

This point is much like a general goal, and if it is understood, participants are much more likely to be specific about goals and strategies. Understanding that the school is a source and reinforcer of racial attitudes is a prerequisite for doing something about it.

4. *Direct study of prejudice and racism, as well as studies that are relevant to minority cultures, should be an integral part of the regular curriculum and should not be isolated as a one-time experience.* Again, this is a general point which emphasizes the content and context of education provided in a school. Attitudes and behavior are shaped by minute-to-minute, day-in and day-out happenings in a school. Understanding this will help participants set specific goals and design strategies for change.

One reason why racial stereotypes are institutionalized is that teachers, both minority and white, tend to expect less from minority students. This general but pervasive point will affect many of the goals set in the next chapter.

5. *Since we have defined racism and seen that our attitudes are negative, let's assume that racism exists and see what we can do about it.* This is the essence of the transitional link between theory and practice that this chapter provides. If participants understand this, they are indeed ready to move on. Even if everyone is not convinced, we ask them to assume that racism exists. Obviously, some people will never be convinced, but if enough people understand, they will tend to draw the others along into the final stages.

6

Changing Behavior: What Can Be Done

THE NATURE OF GOALS

A person or institution that has moved through the previous stages of the model should be ready to get down to business, which, as we know by now, is to begin *doing* something about racism. But before we attempt to jump in and start to shake things up, we need to know what our specific goals are. Failure to do this has been the undoing of more than one do-gooder. Thus we will expand upon Chapter 1's five key points about goals.

Goals must be stated so as to provide directions for change. This point sounds simple but it is often overlooked. Without stated goals, energy and action become misdirected and random, and effective change does not take place. With the background of the earlier chapters, it should be possible to state desired outcomes or goals which work against racism.

The more clearly we know what we are striving for, the more likely we are to accomplish it.

Goals should be as specific and operational as possible. Following this principle will help us avoid the "umbrella" goal, such as "eliminating racism in our school," and substitute a series of subgoals, such as "increase the number of black teachers" and "incorporate the contributions of minorities in the Chemistry I curriculum."

A behavioral goal is measurable and observable. For instance, "reduce the number of reported incidents of problems between black and white students" is preferable to "improve the interracial atmosphere in the school." The former is more specific and observable than the latter.

Strategies are separate from goals in that they are ways of accomplishing goals. Being able to separate means from ends is the issue here. In fact, failure to understand this relationship may be the greatest contributor to racism and many other societal problems. Many of our social institutions were established for fairly benign, if not benevolent, purposes.

However, *it is when the perpetuation of an institution, rather than its original purpose, becomes an end in itself that we have a problem.* For instance, our legal system developed as a means of equitably resolving disputes between individuals or collections of individuals, and it probably served this function in its inception. However, when the major goal becomes preserving the system itself, the goal itself is formidable. Those who cry for "law and order," regardless of the effects of those laws, are confusing ends and means—although we recognize that maintaining an unjust legal system may well be the goal of some people. As originally designed, however, the legal system was a strategy for accomplishing the goal of resolving disputes fairly.

Whenever a strategy becomes a goal, the seeds of institutional discrimination are sown. Perhaps another example will help clarify the point. To accomplish the broad goal of combating institutional racism at the University of Maryland —and such specific subgoals as increasing black student enrollment and student and faculty knowledge of racism—a group called the Campus Coalition Against Racism (CCAR) was formed (both authors served as leaders in this group). For several years the group accomplished many things, including the objectives noted above. However, as older students graduated and the racism issue was replaced by opposition to the war in Vietnam and/or ecology—vital issues to many students —interest in CCAR waned. The biggest choice came when some members of the group wished to shift its focus from knotty racial issues to more broadly based human relations, getting-to-know-each other issues. This was suggested *in order to keep the group together*. Thus CCAR, which originally operated as a strategy, was in danger of becoming a goal. We suggested that the group disband, which it did, because a strategy should not become an end in itself. For the effective agent for change, all strategies (institutions) are "up for grabs" at all times.

Goals must be adjusted to the context of the times.   This relates to the above point about strategies. While enrolling more minorities in primarily white colleges and universities may have been an appropriate goal for the 1970s, it may be totally inappropriate for the 1980s. If, hypothetically, compelling evidence should become available that blacks do better in society by attending all-black schools, the racism fighter of the 1980s would try to keep blacks out of most of our colleges and universities.

Thus you should work hard to accomplish those goals you have set, but always be willing to seek new information. (This key strategy point will be discussed in the next chapter.) Basically, we are proposing a "probability" model of action. Work hardest on, and give most attention to, those goals that are most important and effective in eliminating racism. Do not "fight to the death" on all issues.

As an example of the probability model of action, let us take the case of a high school which was considering installing a course in Swahili for its black students. On the surface the idea sounded good, but when various facts about the proposal came out, its "good idea" probability was only 50–50. Because the plan would have allowed blacks to take the course in lieu of regular English, opponents argued that this would deny black students a chance to learn or improve their English-language skills. And, as one opponent put it: "How many job applications have you seen in Swahili?" Thus while the proposed program might have provided some cultural enrichment for black students, it would have denied them some of their right to a basic education. This goal needed restating before we were ready to push hard for it.

It should also be made clear that probabilities must ultimately be determined by you, as the change agent, individually. Obviously, many well-intended people, all working for the elimination of racism, will see things differently. We hope, then, that our book will provide a common basis for action and reduce the number of opposing actions. Even if the reader does not agree with all our proposals, we hope that it will generate some improvement in our ability to deal with racism.

All goals must be evaluated as to the extent of their accomplishment.   Once you have stated the goals, be sure that you later assess their degree of accomplishment, both large and small. It is easy to remember only the successes and forget the failures. Nevertheless, the converse often occurs with those who are concerned with change: we dwell on our failures and forget our successes. The best change agent, however, optimizes his or her successes and analyzes and learns from failures. It is difficult to be realistic, but that is what is required.

Notice that *degree* of accomplishment is emphasized.

Ideally, we have clearly stated goals and clear accomplishments, or lack thereof: yes or no, good or bad. But, unfortunately, results are often hard to evaluate. For instance, let us say our goal was to increase the number of blacks on a staff by 10 percent and only a 5 percent gain was achieved. We should be able to consider that as a partial success, and, of course, as a partial failure.

Because evaluation is often poorly done in human relations or race-related programs, we would like to offer a general approach to evaluation which we have employed on a number of occasions. The first category for evaluation is *information*: What have participants learned as a result of our program or actions? In conferences it is possible to develop a paper-and-pencil multiple choice or open-ended recall-type test to measure knowledge about racism, such as (1) Define *institutional* and *individual* racism. (2) Cite three examples of institutional racism: (a) in your school, (b) in your town, (c) in the society at large.

A second area of evaluation is *attitudinal change*, in which we commonly employ the SAS "before and after." Ideally, there is a control group to check results against. A third evaluation is whether specific *outcome goals*, both long and short term, were accomplished. This is, of course, the focus of most of this chapter. A more preliminary consideration is whether goals were at least stated. A fourth category which we recommend, particularly if you are evaluating the work of others or grant-supported programs, is to allow the program manager to provide *additional objective evidence* on behalf of the program's accomplishments. This leaves it open to new ideas, and also to critics who say, "You just can't evaluate my program that way." But note that we ask for *objective evidence*. "Gut" reactions are useless to the serious change agent. Most programs and most goals for change can fit the above categories. We recommend applying these categories or criteria to all the change work you encounter, be it yours or that of others. Obviously, not all the categories apply to all goals, but all goals should fit somewhere in the evaluation scheme.

Examples of Goals

While many different goals could be stated, the balance of this chapter will deal with a number of goals we have seen employed in various contexts. The rationale for each goal will also be discussed. Chapter 7 will discuss specific strategies that could be employed to accomplish each goal.

1. *Change the concept of teacher quotas and develop a fair policy.*   Although the term "quota" has often been abused in race relations, here is another good place to be "behavioral." Whether it is called a quota, a target or a goal, we believe that specific numbers or percentages of minority teachers and students should be stated and work should commence in achieving that outcome. Quite often the percentage goal can reflect the percentage of minorities in the state or school district.

It is often argued, however, that it is unfair to state percentages and that hiring should be on a "whoever is qualified and applies" basis. The problem with this is that many forms of institutional racism prevent minorities from finishing high school or going to college, and even from applying for jobs in some school districts.

Thus the institutional racism that has caused a shortage of minority teachers will continue if it is not boldly attacked, and setting a specific goal can dramatize an issue and force change. Thus fairness, which is the elimination of institutional racism, is *not* equal access in a racist context.

Fairness in student selection in higher education was discussed in Chapter 3, and the same principles apply to selection for jobs. We are not suggesting that unqualified people be hired, but we *are* suggesting that "qualifications" are often culturally biased. People should be hired in keeping with their *most appropriate qualifications,* based on their cultural-racial background. A further discussion of qualifications can be found on p. 53.

2. *Integrate minority and racism-related content in the curriculum.* Rather than set up a "Black Week," integrate an ongoing program on the contributions, feelings, and lifestyles of minorities into the curriculum. Also, the facts about racism, both individual and institutional, should be presented in context.

A great source of difficulty here is that much of the curricula is affected by the *way* teachers present the formal material and—even more important—by the informal material teachers present. If teachers present formal content in a half-hearted or uninformed manner, students will be quick to turn off and lose interest. Also, the way teachers react informally to racial issues and events, to minority students in the classroom and cafeteria, etc., communicates a great deal to students, both minority and white.

3. *Instigate effective preplanning and programming in newly desegregated schools.* While "effective" is a less than ideal behavioral term, it means applying the model (or something similar) to a school *before troubles begin.* Teachers, administrators, and students in many newly integrated schools deny the various problems or get "hung up" in Stages I or II. By glossing over the issues, individuals who are directly and indirectly connected with the school do not prepare to deal with racism, and troubles eventually break out.

Another common mistake is to focus on the physical aspects of the change, such as busing patterns, teacher transfers, and class schedules. A smooth physical change is a prerequisite for effective desegregation, but it is not enough.

A related problem in a newly desegregated school is "Do

it once and forget it," whereas an ongoing program is impera-
tive, including reorientation *each year*. Students, teachers, and
staff come and go, and just because things went well last year
does not mean the "new crop" will not need help.

4. *Eliminate inappropriate discipline.*   A common situation in many schools is that whites and blacks receive different forms of discipline. In some schools a tighter rein is
applied to blacks, and they are usually blamed when trouble
starts. However, in many schools the opposite condition exists:
blacks are relatively undisciplined compared to whites. Either
situation is racist.

If blacks receive more severe discipline, they will resent
it and will cause all the more trouble. Consequently the school
will "come down" even harder, and a spiraling effect will
occur. Also, when these students leave school they are likely
to continue the pattern, and in a white-dominated society, the
black who has "a chip on his or her shoulder" is bound to lose.

Conversely, if blacks are undisciplined, they form an unrealistic picture of how to get along with others, particularly
whites and authority figures, and are unlikely to be prepared
for life outside the school.

5. *Change the use of standardized test scores.*   This has
been discussed previously, particularly in Chapter 3. Note that
the emphasis is on changing *the use* of test scores rather than
the elimination of tests. Strategies to accomplish this will be
discussed in the next chapter.

6. *Find ways of involving minority students' parents in
school affairs.*   Whereas many schools have trouble involving
even majority parents in school affairs, minority parents often
have even less input. *Thus particular and unique efforts must
be made to involve minority parents* or, by default, we end up
with a system that has only white input.

Minority parents may be either actively or passively

turned away from the school. Remember, institutional racism need not be intentional. Unfortunately, many school officials say they want to have minority parent input but appear to do everything to discourage it.

7. *Make sure there is follow-up after a conference or workshop.* Many a good beginning has been viewed by participants and/or administrators as an end in itself. Even the most successful conference has only a limited effect if a specific follow-up procedure is not planned and executed.

8. *Develop proper techniques for teaching standard English to black youngsters, while making sure that their native speech style is not put down in the process.* Again, recognition of cultural and racial differences begins this cycle (which was covered in Chapter 2). If teachers understand that they are working with a variety of races and cultures and that their job is not so much to force everyone into the same mold as to give everyone the relevant tools for success, we will have made great strides. Indeed, the basic meaning of the word "education" is to develop the potential in each person. This is best done in terms of the students' culture and background.

9. *Achieve central administration support for positions that are taken to reduce or eliminate racism.* Obtaining direct and indirect support on racism-related issues can release a great deal of energy in the system. This is not the only route to action, but those who are in formal power positions in an organization must eventually be part of the change process.

10. *Find appropriate standards for judging and developing programs for blacks in a positive way.* If we understand that cultural and racial differences exist, it is logical to conclude that we need different techniques and criteria to judge success or failure. The testing issue is an appropriate example.

It is not suggested that we lower standards of admission to college, only that we use the most appropriate standards for any given group. If a separate measure or test gives us a better indication of how a student will perform, it is unfair to use another standard.

11. *Experience and understanding of racism and race relations should be required of all school personnel*—a simply stated but sweeping goal. This becomes a statement of the qualifications for working in a school, just as a college degree is for teachers or experience in food preparation is for cafeteria workers.

12. *Black artists and scholars should be included in the curricula.* Not only does this have important role-modeling implications for black students, it shows white and black students that blacks can and do perform many important roles in society. It also serves as an intermediate goal on the way to acquiring more full-time black faculty members. If black consultants can be brought in on a temporary or part-time basis, and if this is done properly, such a program can have a strong impact on a school.

7

Changing Behavior: How It Can Be Done

While the previous chapter dealt with goals in general, this chapter will concentrate on the strategies one might employ in accomplishing a given goal. Because there is no *one* way to accomplish a given goal, the good social strategist has a variety of methods and techniques available at all times. A simple example of this is a typical speaking engagement, as we are called upon frequently to make presentations at schools, before PTAs, neighborhood groups, campus organizations, and so forth. A good speaker, we've found, tries to determine in advance who will be in the audience, how large the group will be, the physical arrangements (e.g., an auditorium or a small room), and any special interests the group might have. However, new conditions often arise that necessitate a change in strategy. For instance, on one occasion the senior author was asked to "meet informally" with a few teachers about what they might do about racism in their school, but upon arrival it turned out that the plans had been changed and the new format called for a formal address to an overflow PTA meeting that had been called to discuss the issue—complete with irate parents. Obviously, the presentation one would give in an auditorium to 350 highly emotional people differs from what one would give to a small group of teachers. On another occasion we were called upon to run a three-hour workshop session for a group of teachers, but just before we began we were told that we had only an hour and a half.

Several lessons from these examples are worth noting. First, no matter how informal or unstructured the occasion may be, *the effective change agent must be prepared for many contingencies.* He or she is prepared not only for the highest-probability event (the expected) but also for the unexpected. Controlling the situation and keeping in mind that you are trying to influence and change others are important principles. If you are working toward specific goals, keep them in mind and seize every opportunity to implement them. (A talk to a group about racism is one implementation of the model.)

Probably the best general advice—after you feel comfortable with this or any other model—is to derive the utmost experience from such occasions: set goals, develop strategies, and evaluate outcomes. The greater the variety of conditions you experience, the more able you will be to handle emergencies and still accomplish your goals.

Another key ingredient of effective change is *self-confidence,* as critics are likely to say, "Why are you always so negative?" or "What makes you think you are so right all the time?" An effective change agent, of course, should have answers for these and many other questions. Moreover, many of those who accuse you of being negative are not likely to face problems realistically. But racism requires a solution, and if it is never realistically diagnosed as a problem, it will never be solved. Thus the effective change agent uses the model as a pragmatic solution, not as something to feel emotional about, one way or the other; and the model is only as good as its outcomes. Actually, few people are as optimistic as an effective change agent, for he or she believes, and regularly demonstrates, that things can get better, that change is possible, that effort in behalf of change is worthwhile. This is hardly a negative position.

The other criticism ("What makes you so right?") should also be pragmatically countered. Right is what works; wrong is what doesn't work. The reason you think you are right is that you have evidence that your strategy works, and you are perfectly willing to alter the strategy if it fails. Thus the system is open and honest.

You will find that most critics do not have practical alternatives to offer, nor do they have any system of operating. But if their arguments and evidence make sense, change your strategy. However, remember that *the only test of a strategy is whether it works.*

We are sure some readers are saying, "Wait a minute; are you saying the end justifies the means?" Not quite. We are saying that the change agent should ask, *"Does this particular end justify this particular means?"*

Most of us would risk extreme measures to achieve greater outcomes. For instance, to what extremes would you go to save your own life? the life of a stranger? the life of an animal or a flower? All of us operate with different probability systems. That is, we operate with different evaluations for accomplishing a given goal. Thus we do not advocate particular strategies or goals for others; we can only report on how we see things and what we have done in given circumstances. We have not fully tested our limits on what we would or wouldn't use as strategies.

An open system, where strategies are considered good or

bad or acceptable or unacceptable only in relation to a particular goal, has much to recommend it. For one thing, it helps vanquish a classic bugaboo of the change agent: artificial self-limitations. *Most limitations to effective change are self-imposed.* This sweeping statement says that since it is not my boss, my husband, or the President who is holding me back, it must be *me*.

An analogy is an interpretation of the United States Constitution. If we view the Constitution as a document which tells us only what is allowable, we are what is popularly labeled a "strict constructionist." But if we view the Constitution as a document that tells us only what we *can't* do, then the range of things we *can* do is enormous. Therefore, do not place more restrictions on your behavior than are necessary to accomplish your goals. Thus the effective change agent has a much greater repertoire of behavior than the average citizen.

If we draw another analogy—to a card game—the average citizen simply plays the cards he or she is dealt; no questions are asked, and the game and the rules are given. If the black players get only three cards and the white players five—well, that's the way it goes. The change agent is also in the minority, but he or she asks what game it is, who set up the rules, how many new cards each player gets—and, most importantly, he or she also tries to get possession of the deck and change it, as well as the dealer. Most people simply go along with things as they are, so that if we change the deck and the game from racist to nonracist, people will tend to play by the new rules. New generations, in turn, will play the non-racist game from the start.

This is probably the best general argument for concentrating on institutional change rather than individual change, for it would take much longer to persuade each player, one at a time, to ask for a new deck than to get possession of the deck and change it. Many strategists would disagree, but we have found that institutional change generally has a greater probability of payoff per unit of energy expended. This is not to say, however, that we would reject any strategy or model employed by others. Many people may be more comfortable and effective in a one-to-one situation. Indeed, most of our counselors and personnel workers work with individuals rather than groups.

What we are saying is that *more people are capable of affecting institutions than ever give it a try.* Most laypersons and professional social scientists think of people and behavior problems in single units, but there is much evidence to suggest that this approach is too molecular to solve human problems. And we really can't see the forest if we look at it one tree at a time. We also recognize that a long-term effective social change requires the efforts of many people operating in different ways. Thus when we are asked "Do you agree with so-and-so's tactics?" our only response is to ask whether they worked or not. There are no inherently good or bad strategies.

Alinsky (1971) provided us with a great deal of practical information about the art and science of change. In addition to some of the points cited above, he developed others. One interesting point he discussed is that *effective action requires that a change be viewed as "moral" by its proponents.* Defining an issue in terms of "good guys" and "bad guys," or right and wrong, is a useful strategy. You may not believe that your side is all right and the other side is all wrong, but sharpening the issue in those terms can be effective. (No one ever went to war because his or her side was felt to be 60 percent right and 40 percent wrong.) This ploy is relatively easy to use in most racist situations: playing up the underdog—the powerless minority that is exploited by the system and the powers that run it.

Alinsky also mentions the *value of dramatizing your situation with a tactic that has no direct connection with a given goal.* Discussing a strategy he employed to get officials of the city of Chicago to deliver on some changes they promised to make in a certain neighborhood, Alinsky proposed to tie up all the washroom facilities at Chicago's O'Hare Airport simply by keeping them occupied with members of the neighborhood organization. This, he reasoned, would cause anxiety among the incoming passengers, mothers with small children, etc., and create such general paralysis in the airport as to be a huge headache for city officials. Would the city send the police to raid the washrooms and drag people out from the stalls? How could they tell the protesters from the nonprotesters? By leaking the story, Alinsky's group achieved a quick reversal of the position taken by city hall, and the promised changes were quickly forthcoming. But, as he noted in his book, his group was prepared to go through with the strategy.

Let us analyze this example in terms of several principles noted by Alinsky, as well as some additional points. First, a desirable trait for any change agent is a demonstrated irreverence for social institutions. *If you respect too many "sacred cows," you are unnecessarily limiting your potential strategies.* The example also employs strategies that are unfamiliar to the people one is trying to change. The airport and city officials probably would not have known what to do and would have "lost their cool" in the confusion. Therefore, if a tactic is within the experience of those you are changing, it can be handled easily by the latter and thus does not serve the purpose of change.

For instance, when campus demonstrations were first employed, they were effective because they were outside the experience of college and university administrators. However, once administrators learned how to deal with them, demonstrations were no longer effective.

Another lesson from the O'Hare example is that a threatened strategy need not actually be carried out to be effective. However, the people you are trying to influence must perceive that it is probable that you will carry out the strategy. And the more negatively they view the outcome, the lower the probability level required to induce action. Thus it follows: *One must always be prepared to carry out a bluff.* Anyone who has ever had a child call his or her bluff knows the consequences of not being prepared to follow through.

A last point about the Alinsky example is that a tactic can also be fun. Change agents often view the process of developing strategies as grim warfare whereas, in fact, *strategies which are humorous or enjoyable are often more effective than serious ones.*

J. W. Gardner (1971) has developed a set of eight rules for effective action which he uses in his citizens' lobby, Common Cause. His first rule is that *effective action must be a full-time and continuing effort.* Unpredictable waxing and waning of enthusiasm will have little effect on deeply rooted institutional racism.

His second rule is to *limit the number of targets and hit them hard.* This is compatible with our probability model and guards against the dissipation of energy by having too broad a focus or target. His third rule is to *use professionals wherever possible.* This guards against the impression that enthusiasm is enough to win battles. Working with people who know the system and how to beat it is important. His fourth rule is to *form alliances.* Banding groups together for related causes can help accomplish multiple goals.

Gardner's fifth rule is to *tell the story.* Effective communication is the most powerful weapon to use against special-interest groups. Mass media, letters to congressmen, and so forth result in an aroused public. The sixth rule is that *active, dedicated workers are preferable to large numbers of workers.* Active workers spread their influence by reaching out in the community. His seventh rule is *make allies in the institution one is trying to change.* If you assume that everyone is against you, you will alienate valuable resources. The eighth rule is *organize for action.* Many groups talk of action but are geared for study, discussion, or education. In effect, this book is dedicated to this eighth rule.

In another of his works Gardner (1965) discusses the need for flexible, self-renewing institutions. That is, institutions should be changed in such a way that the primary goal is to make them self-changing on a regular basis. If we are only able to move an institution from one specific or static point to another, we will constantly be in trouble. Additionally, in our rapidly changing society the chances of institutions keeping pace without built-in self-renewal mechanisms are remote.

Nader (1971), one of the most successful change agents in America, focuses on economic issues that relate to consumer protection and extends them to include their effects on racism. For instance, he develops the point that blacks, on average, are exposed to more health-damaging pollutants than whites because blacks tend to live in inner-city or ghetto areas. The same negative situation exists for blacks in most economic areas, such as lower quality and higher prices for the products that are available to them, victimization by loan sharks, and so forth. Nader's change tactics revolve around identification of the problem, research, public exposure, use of legal methods, and community action.

Nader (1972) has also developed a useful strategy called a Public Interest Research Group (PIRG). Members of these statewide groups (mostly college students) donate $3 per year to hire full-time advocates, lawyers, researchers, etc., to examine community needs and work for change. Nader sees this strategy as replacing the large demonstrations and fragmented student activities of the 1960s. He feels it will keep students interested and involved with community concerns.

This strategy is much like a statewide Common Cause, as developed by Gardner.

Downs (1970) also develops a number of strategies for combating racism in the society as a whole. His strategies, largely economic, are aimed at changing the behavior of whites and increasing the capabilities of nonwhites. His strategies are basically compatible with those developed earlier in this chapter.

The last point we will make about strategies is that we can't tell you exactly what to do under all conditions. We can lay down principles, and describe what we have done, but it remains for each person to apply those principles in his or her particular and unique situation. The good change agent will have made a thorough analysis of the situation to discover what will work, or what will reinforce, harass, or transcend the experience of those he or she is trying to change.

CAN YOU USE RESEARCH TO MAKE A DIFFERENCE?

Undoubtedly, research in any field has sometimes had a direct and relatively immediate effect. At other times, differences may appear much later and be unknown to the researchers. As journals are published, reports circulated, and presentations given, researchers are seldom provided with direct feedback on how their data have influenced the policies, practices, or even the research of others.

But researchers' uses of data are often *passive* and require that action or reaction be initiated by others in pursuing the findings of research, whereas this section deals with the *active* use of data to initiate change or to influence others. The Cultural Study Center, begun at the University of Maryland, College Park, in 1969 for conducting intercultural and race-related research, aimed at making changes in the educational system and the larger society. The Center has generated many studies, but its staff must continually ask the question, Have we changed anything? While change can take many forms, we were particularly concerned with reducing and eliminating institutional racism. The following are two fairly clear-cut examples of change that resulted directly from research data. Admittedly, it is difficult to determine if the outcomes would have been the same without the research, since there were no control conditions or groups, but the circumstances provide rather direct evidence of the role of research in eliminating racism.

The first example concerns altered admission policies. The University of Maryland had for some years employed minimum entrance requirements for in-state students: a C average and graduation from high school. Students were required to take the SAT, but these scores were used for placement, not selection. Faced with increased applications and insufficient facilities and services, the Board of Regents devised a policy that would incorporate the SAT and the high school grade-point average in a single, weighted statistical equation for all entering freshmen, regardless of race or sex, using predicted end-of-year freshman grades as a criterion.

The equation was developed by another research office on the campus and was competently done, as far as it went. However, this office had not considered race-sex subgroup differences, such as bias in the predictors, different weights in the equation for each subgroup, or alternative predictors for subgroups. But the Cultural Study Center, which had conducted research on these topics, provided it to the Regents and the central administration. However, the use of the data was passive in that it required synthesis and reaction by the decision makers. Even though we felt the Center's data strongly indicated that a single statistical equation would be inappropriate and unfair to blacks, the decision had been made otherwise.

It seemed that we had a classic example of institutional

racism in the revised admission policy. The results of our studies (see Chapter 3) indicated that fewer blacks would be accepted and that irrelevant selection procedures were being employed under the new policy. Armed with these data, we set upon an active course and we worked with many individuals, groups, and coalitions to convince them of the soundness of our data and position. These groups included (among others) the central administrators, the black faculty and staff, the admissions staff, black students, white students, a coalition group of students, and interested faculty and staff. We strategically employed many roles to pull these elements together around our position. Many of those who disagreed with the announced policy shared our concern but could offer no logical, pragmatic alternatives.

Possession of the kinds of research data cited above enabled us to take a strong position and suggest practical solutions to the dilemma. Ultimately, through developing the power bases in those groups and "speaking softly but carrying a big stick," one of us was appointed to a committee of faculty members and administrators that had been formed to advise the central administration. As a result of the report of this committee, the central administration recommended that the Board of Regents reverse its decision, which it did. The new decision was that freshmen could be admitted by a statistical equation (including the SAT) or another equation that used only a high school grade-point average and class rank. Additionally, 104 students would be selected for the fall term on the basis of the alternative predictors we had developed in our research, which consisted of nontraditional measures of accomplishment relevant to minority cultures.

We found that successful blacks tended to be independent, self-assured, and confident that they can change their lives by their own efforts. They understand how society operates; they expect racism and are prepared to deal with it; and they will have achieved some form of success outside the classroom.

While the admission decision was not ideal from our perspective, it was a practical alternative, and it led the institution to alter its position and work against institutional racism. It was only one battle in a large campaign, but we felt we were able to demonstrate the active and practical use of data to promote change.

The second example involves using data to promote curricular change at the university level. Adding or changing courses is one of the most laborious and difficult processes in higher education, and, despite great breastbeating and ballyhoo, the courses that are available for training counselors and personnel workers have changed little in the last decade. This is particularly true in the racial area. Courses on the teaching or counseling of blacks or minorities are beginning to appear in curricula, but this, at best, solves only half the problem. Most whites have little, if any, exposure to or contact with their own racism and prejudice, whether institutional or individual. Thus courses on white racism also are important. Logically, material on racism should be part of nearly all the courses in a curriculum.

The futility of altering the behavior of white personnel workers toward black students without dealing with white racism seemed obvious to us. There was no course at the University of Maryland which personnel workers were likely to take which dealt even superficially with racism. If some readers doubt the usefulness of a course in eliminating racism, the ultimate answer is whether people who take such a course *do something differently* as a result. We felt that emphasizing the principles discussed in this book, focusing on change-agent behavior in class, and requiring antiracism activity outside class were practical approaches to accomplishing change.

We set about developing and trying out curriculum material, such as lecture notes, handouts, and projects, through seminars, workshops, and experimental courses. After acquiring experience in this area, we approached an academic administrator about initiating a course on racism for educators. The administrator refused to consider the course, even on a special topics basis, even though it would be taught by one of his own faculty members, who was also a member of the Cultural Study Center staff. The stated reason for his opposition was primarily his skepticism about the viability of racism, and particularly racism in education, as a legitimate academic topic. He considered racism left-wing "pop" sociology and asked, "What good would it do to tell someone they are racists for sixteen weeks?" He also professed doubt that there was any racism in the educational system worth discussing.

We too had asked ourselves similar questions some years earlier, but we had set about answering them through research. Our research on the Situational Attitude Scale (SAS) was discussed in detail in Chapter 4. We also developed many of the examples of racism used in Chapter 3, such as biased admission standards, white-oriented student activities, and the limited number of courses relevant to blacks. These data, with our instructional materials, more than supported the contention that racism exists, that it is measurable and operational, and that it takes many complex forms, including some that are peculiar to education and educators.

Through the work of interested graduate students and faculty, several levels of barriers to adoption of the course were eliminated and the course was presented in such a way as to make it of self-evident value to the university. As of this writing, the course, called Education and Racism, is still being offered, and further work is being done to make it a required course. (This book provides the structure for the Education and Racism course.)

Students are not only required to know the material but

they are expected to conduct individual and group projects outside the classroom. Another course requirement, which has worked well, is to keep a log of examples of racism encountered by students during the semester. These incidents are discussed and analyzed in writing and in class. This forces students to be conscious of the racism around them, and often results in surprise or shock about examples in their families or on their jobs. A discussion of the material from the course and in this book is available on audiotape (see Sedlacek, 1974).

These two examples are briefly stated, but they involved many complexities and problems. Also, they show that it is possible for research to make a real difference in contemporary and controversial issues. Whether the gains outweigh the losses, or whether the results can be generalized, is hard to determine. However, several overall conclusions seem warranted.

First, *the context in which data are used is critical.* In both situations the persons who pushed for the changes were able to organize and alter the components in the environment so that the data could be used. A research staff that has not had comparable, routine involvement in many segments of campus or community life would find it much more difficult to bring about change than we did. But whatever situation a change agent finds, sophistication and knowledge about the system one is trying to change are mandatory.

Second, *size does not appear to be critical,* since the Cultural Study Center has limited funds and only one full-time researcher. Additionally, the Center is part of the Division of Student Affairs, which is relatively powerless to produce changes in academic affairs. Thus a change mechanism that has little formal power can acquire what it needs through informal means. Indeed, an important part of the Education and Racism course deals with developing and using power to effect change.

The third important principle that is demonstrated by the change in admission procedures is willingness to compromise. *A good change agent is willing to compromise for the best that can be achieved.* Again, pragmatism. The person who holds out for perfection, when there is little if any chance of success, does his or her goal a disservice. Compromise requires strength, not weakness. If you can get only one-third of your goal, you are better off than when you started; and you can always come back to get the other two-thirds.

This brings up another stratagem that is also used in other types of negotiations: *asking for more than you want but settling for what you really wanted.* This tactic can backfire if it is overused, but it worked in the admission case cited above. Although we had asked for it, we did not expect to select 104 students, but we accepted this provision when it was offered.

It should also be noted that both examples involved changes outside the Division of Student Affairs: one in central administration and the other in an academic unit.

Fourth, it is important that expertise be developed in some fashion; and in this case our research was most crucial. *Developing power by becoming the only viable source of information on a topic is critical.*

Fifth, *power should not be used directly, if this can be avoided.* The more it can be made to appear that the institution itself, or the individuals within it, brought about the change, the more likely the chance of success. The "big stick" will have to be used every once in a while, but an eye should be kept on the goal: on change rather than on the method, and on the exercise of power and influence through research. Our "big stick" was pressure from a variety of sources, on and off campus, and the threat or potential of dramatizing the issue throughout the state and in the media. The administration wished to avoid this.

Another important point is *to select goals for change that can realistically be accomplished.* Fighting the good fight, losing, and nevertheless feeling good about it is detrimental to change in the long run. The wrong result is positively reinforced. Results, not intentions, are the mark of success. High expectations for realistic change is the desirable philosophy. Thus we did not try to include all branches of the university in our goals in the above examples; we felt we could accomplish change on the main campus and worry about the others later.

Ultimately, it will require efforts by many individual researchers, counselors, personnel workers, and educators to alter institutional racism in the educational system and the larger society. The role of a change agent is beginning to be discussed in many quarters as a viable, perhaps prototypical model for educators and personnel workers (Sedlacek and Brooks, 1973b; Sedlacek and Horowitz, 1974).

EXAMPLES OF STRATEGIES

At this point we would like to take the goals in Chapter 6 and discuss specific strategies for accomplishing them.

1. *Change the concept of teacher quotas and develop a fair policy.* One strategy which has been employed with some success on several occasions by us and by others is to provide an accurate account of the percentage of minority teachers and to compare it to the percentage of minority students in the municipality, state, or district. This information was then circulated to the appropriate officials and the disproportion was shown to be racist, in effect if not intention. Minority teacher-recruiting programs were subsequently begun in several schools, but there was always a temptation to consider these programs as ends in themselves. More determined and unusual methods of recruiting are often needed in an institu-

tional system that has a negative or neutral reputation among blacks.

Visits to black colleges, black churches, black community centers, and to the black media can also be helpful. More extreme strategies include teacher or student strikes, newspaper, TV and radio coverage that dramatizes the issue, and demonstrations. These tactics can be employed to highlight the policy that only minority teachers be hired until the quota is reached. Always encourage others to take a position which is more severe and militant than yours, and your position—by comparison—will then seem reasonable.

As noted before, every serious social movement in history has employed a wide range of strategies to accomplish its ends, and the elimination of racism is no exception. Legal recourse should also be used. Many a significant antiracism development has included a legal battle.

2. *Integrate minority- and racism-related content into the curriculum.* A key strategy here is to encourage serious in-service teacher training. Instructional materials must be developed, but the goal is to have teachers understand and use the material. While curricula are being developed in specialty areas, such as social studies, a few schools are considering introducing minority-relevant content throughout their curricula. Additionally, very few schools deal systematically with racism as content. Optimally, however, teachers must cover race-related issues in both the formal and informal context of their interactions with pupils.

For instance, a teacher reported that when he was taping some student interviews in a hallway for an English class, someone used the word "nigger." The teacher was unsure of what he should do, but eventually he edited the word out and avoided the topic in class. But it would have been better had he played the original tape in class and turned it into a lesson on racism. Discussing why the remark was made, and its implications, would have been useful and realistic, and the students could see that their teacher was not deliberately avoiding the topic. The issue could have been discussed as it occurred as well as in the English class.

A strategy that worked particularly well in a conference we conducted at a secondary school was assigning teachers to do something to fight racism with their students and then report back on their efforts. Having to make a report is an effective way to initiate real action. A typing teacher, for example, had her class type material on racism and turned the students' reactions into a lesson. A chemistry teacher, who discussed the composition of a hair straightener used by blacks, got into a discussion of why many more blacks resorted to this process in the past than in the present. This is good in-context teaching.

3. *Instigate effective preplanning and programming in newly desegregated schools.* Getting school personnel to act preventively about racism is difficult, particularly in schools which are newly desegregated. Sounding the alarm by describing problems that have occurred in other schools may help. For the particularly lethargic school with latent racial problems, it may be beneficial to stir things up a bit by working with change-oriented student or parent groups or to generate a mild confrontation to dramatize the issues. The confrontation could take a variety of forms, including letters, demonstrations, and boycotts. This is tricky business, and could easily backfire. However, we suggest that it not be ruled out without consideration.

This strategy, of course, has been a favorite of dictators and despots throughout history: artificially dramatizing a need for their services and organizing people for action on the rebound. However, if racism did not exist, there would be no situation to dramatize. It is nevertheless important to keep goals and strategies separate. Although Hitler was an effective organizer and strategist, we need not share his goals to use one of his methods. *Strategies exist independently of the nature of the goal and the personality of the strategist.*

A word might also be said about the words "desegregate" and "integrate" and the many positive and negative connotations given to each term. But more important than semantics are the operational definitions. We use "desegregate" to describe the physical intermingling of whites and minorities, without qualitative connotations or evaluations. The word "integrate" could be used to effect our ideal society and educational system, so far as racism is concerned. We feel that a multiracial and multicultural environment—where different groups are allowed to mix or separate as they wish in expressing their lifestyles, but where no one suffers negative consequences because of his or her individual or collective choice —is a desirable, nonracist condition. If you choose to call that integration, fine. If not, choose your own term.

One point that is often overlooked in the newly desegregated school is that many people (other than teachers and administrators) regularly interact with students and can make or break the new situation. Parents, community residents, bus drivers, cafeteria workers, custodial staff, the school board, etc., must all be part of any antiracism training program. Chesler (1971), who provides a number of suggestions for approaching racism in a newly desegregated school, delineates targets of change or retraining, such as students, teachers, and community members, and provides examples of strategies for change for each group. His strategies include written and audiovisual materials, laboratory training sessions, and problem-solving teams. He points out that his strategies cannot stand by themselves; they must be combined in order to attack racist structures in the schools.

Perhaps this is a good place to raise the issue of busing,

which has been grossly overemphasized by many people, both inside and outside education. We view busing as only one of many strategies that can be employed in desegregating a school, but the pro-racism forces have seized upon busing as their "big" issue in preventing change. Strategically, this is a good tactic from their standpoint because it avoids the issue and cloaks busing in the guise of "neighborhood schools for neighborhood children." Nevertheless, the issue of whether students have a legal right to attend neighborhood schools has been answered in the negative on numerous occasions by the courts, but with little fanfare (U.S. Commission on Civil Rights, 1972).

Providing pupil transportation is nearly as old as public education itself. In 1869 Massachusetts became the first state to provide pupil transportation at public expense, and by 1919 all states did so (this was also the year of the first school bus). Today, nearly half the school children in the United States are bused to school, and only a small part of this is for purposes of desegregation. (U.S. Commission on Civil Rights, 1972.) Indeed, busing has also been used to enforce *segregation*. Blacks and whites have been routinely hauled much greater distances than are presently considered in de-segregation plans, in order to send them to all-black or all-white schools, but this did not elicit strenuous opposition.

In 1972 the U.S. Commission on Civil Rights provided a number of arguments that are useful against opponents of busing. It reported that school buses are forty times safer than private automobiles and four times safer than walking to school. Also, it reported few race-related incidents on buses, and stated that in only two of eleven surveyed cities had the length of the average bus trip increased by more than fifteen minutes since busing for desegregation was instituted. It also reported that, on a national basis, the cost of pupil transportation was 3.5 percent in 1933 and only 3.6 percent of the school budget in 1969/70.

The "antibusing" argument, that it is not the job of the schools to solve racial problems, ignores the long-stated goals of our educational system: preparation for taking an adult role in society. Allowing a segregated educational system to flourish would be to give up any chance of developing a multicultural society in the United States. Some parents, of course, fear for their children, who may be bused into neighborhoods where drugs, crime, and violence flourish. Such fears are well founded, to a certain extent, but all school systems and all parents should be concerned about sending *any* children to schools in such neighborhoods. If we protect whites, but allow blacks and other minorities to attend schools in such neighborhoods, we are supporting an obvious form of institutional racism.

Another way to counter arguments against busing is to challenge opponents to offer alternative proposals to eliminate racism. If there are no viable alternatives, busing should be instituted.

The effective change agent should recognize the emotional climate surrounding this issue and adjust the probabilities of success accordingly. Whether the desegregation of schools and classrooms will increase the performance of minority children (Coleman et al., 1966) or whether the results are inconsistent and more specific (Roberts and Horton, 1973) remains to be seen. However, the great bulk of the evidence in this book suggests that isolating minorities ensures negative outcomes (i.e., inferior education) and is ultimately bad for all of society.

4. *Eliminate inappropriate discipline.* These strategies rely heavily on an understanding and appreciation of cultural and racial differences—by teachers, administrators, and stu-

dents—so that a fair policy can be implemented. Obviously, many school rules and regulations must apply to all students, but *some* rules should not apply to all.

For example, after discussion and analysis of the problems between black and white females in a home economics class, the primary cause was found to be that the white teacher required each girl to wash her hair daily for a unit on good grooming. The black girls, who refused to do this, were threatened with expulsion from the class, and the teacher was at a loss to know why they had refused. We found that washing and properly treating their "natural" hairstyles took considerably longer for the black girls. Neither the teacher, the white girls, nor the black girls had been aware of this difference, and all were resentful. After some explanation and discussion, the class agreed to let the blacks wash their hair twice a week although the whites were still required to wash theirs daily. There was no resentment when everyone understood the situation. Thus differential treatment, rather than identical treatment, was considered appropriate and fair.

A second situation involved physical activity and movement during a school's musical programs. For many blacks, enjoyment of music is routinely accompanied by a great deal of body movement, whereas whites tend to be more outwardly reserved. The principal, upset by the lively movement in the seats during a "soul concert," ruled that everyone was to remain motionless at all assemblies, but the black students resented this and rebelled. After we explained the cultural differences, a final policy was adopted of allowing motion in the seats for *all* students (providing it was not disruptive) but requiring them to remain in their seats. Assemblies and concerts caused no further problems.

The point is that all rules and disciplinary actions should be *interpreted in a cultural context*. It is easy to design rules

a quid pro quo basis, we promised to hold back our data. After he released his statement, progress on the specifics of the report became more rapid.

We were prepared. We had acquired power through the press and campus groups by informal means. And we were prepared to follow through.

10. *Find appropriate standards for judging and developing programs for blacks in a positive way.*   Remember the point we keep coming back to: *equality does not mean everyone is treated in exactly the same way, it means everyone is treated in the most appropriate way, given his or her racial and cultural background.*

In a situation that called for hiring a university center counselor, the current counselors were generally in favor of hiring a black, but only if he or she was qualified. (How often we have heard that statement! Most people feel that qualifications are clearly written on tablets of stone.) Upon probing, we found that the counselors thought "qualified" meant being clinically oriented and having served an internship in a university unit that focused on personal or social problems. It turned out, however, that many black counselors were more interested and better trained in educational counseling than in personal or social counseling and were more likely, therefore, to have served their internship in a community center. Actually, the center needed someone with an educational and community-counseling background who could relate to black students—far more than another white, clinical psychologist. At first the counselors were willing to take only a "white" black, whose training was identical to their own. After explaining these points and lobbying for a particular candidate, we hired a black educational counseling specialist with a community-work background by a 5 to 4 vote of the committee.

11. *Experience and understanding of racism and race*

relations should be required of all school personnel. In-service training programs for the current staff and race relations experience for new personnel are called for here. In hiring a university faculty member, we asked the four top candidates to complete the Situational Attitude Scale and provide evidence of their work on race-related issues. One candidate was flustered and did poorly, and one was annoyed and refused to cooperate. Of the two who complied, one had done a number of positive things in race relations which would not have come out in a typical hiring situation. She got the job.

The important consideration is to get our values "out front" as part of our routine procedures.

12. *Black artists and scholars should be included in the curricula.* This is fairly easily accomplished since it is not a permanent commitment, at least at first. Part-time faculty members from industry, government, or other schools may help "pep up" a curriculum. And it often seems easier to administrators to hire such people than to initiate many of the other changes cited in this book.

Earlier, we discussed how we got a course, Education and Racism, adopted at the University of Maryland. Once it was established, we said we were unavailable to teach it—in order to force the department to bring in someone else with experience in racism. A black female taught the course, and the university had a new, part-time faculty member it would not otherwise have had.

8

The Unique Role Of The Black

Glenwood C. Brooks, Jr.

The title of this chapter implies the special roles a black can play in generating change. However, I will cover the role of the change agent who works within educational systems, at both the pre-college and the college-university level. Such a distinction is necessary in order to sharpen one's awareness of the different strategies that are available to blacks.

The particular strategy outlined in this book depends on using a model that was developed over several years of experience with school systems and experimental studies and that is directed toward all persons (black and white) who find themselves in settings that require consistent hard-nosed solutions but, at the same time, must work with a constituency whose cooperation must be secured. In other words, the model attempts to inform and educate, as a prerequisite to action, but stresses action-oriented solutions with measurable outcomes. At first glance the model may appear to be "softer" and less active than boycotts and demonstrations; as a matter of fact, any kind of strategy—no matter how radical—can be used with the model. The model ensures that, whatever the strategy, it will be employed in optimal circumstances.

The word "change" has been used throughout this book; however, we repeat that by "change" we mean a shift in the social order in American society so that eventually its races and ethnic groups can live without institutional and individual racism. Both forms of racism undermine the nation's potential, depriving it of a large talent pool and rendering only lipservice to its constitutional and moral ideals.

The role of the black in generating change might be that of the black domestic who must work for low wages and carry lunch or a change of clothes in a brown paper bag. Just getting up and going to work suggests a persistence that might be interpreted as a desire—despite all odds—to keep on going. The motion picture *Claudine* (1974) expressed the role of the black domestic eloquently, showing that by going on, by not giving up, the black domestic is acting out change.

A black may also generate change as a college student who feels that he or she must boycott classes to dramatize a grievance against the institution. Or the role might be played by a black radical who is unwilling to seek change within the prescribed forms tolerated by society. The college student and the radical differ from the black domestic in that they seek change purposefully, whereas the lifestyle of the domestic generates change by sheer persistence.

Still another role of the black in generating change is that of the expert with formal knowledge and skills—the consultant. Examples of this role include the human relations officer, the affirmative action officer, the equal opportunity officer, and so forth.

However, whether the change agent is a domestic, a college student, a radical, or a consultant, the role should first be discussed in terms of the psychological dilemmas he or she faces. Psychologically, the role of the black in generating change is full of conflict from within and without. The risk of summary dismissal from a job and the subtle undermining of efforts are ever present. The chances of being misunderstood, if one is even heard, are real and great. Although the black consultant has some tactical advantages because he or she controls agenda to a large extent, and is viewed as an expert, such a consultant is in the ironic position of assisting social change by pointing out his or her oppressed condition directly to the oppressor. In effect, the black consultant, the aggrieved party, advises and works with the aggrievers, who may be ignorant of their attitudes and behavior, or unwilling to alter them. Thus the black risks providing information that the oppressor may well use against him or her or as an excuse to continue with racism.

No respite or recuperative interval exists for blacks, particularly the black consultant, human relations officer, etc., because their role demands either continuous and tension-producing efforts to gain rights and privileges for black Americans and an improved interface with whites or quitting, with the subsequent realization that one has abdicated one's inherent rights and privileges as an American. This, of course, is psychologically damaging. White consultants can always escape from this dilemma, possibly with scars, but the risks for blacks are far greater. Because the physical or financial risks for blacks vary with level of employment and education, the unskilled black who wishes to generate change might be out of a job before the black consultant at the college level who demands a change in racist admission policies. The psychological risks, however, seem to be common across all levels and settings among blacks who participate in generating change.

If one reflects on the roles of the black college student, radical, and consultant, the reader might think that the student and the radical would be grouped in one category and the consultant in another. A convenient label for any change agent's role is "maverick," and the college student and the radical might be considered mavericks. In contrast, the consultant, human relations officer, etc., represents a constituency. The role of the maverick, which is not readily understood by society, is viewed as more "volatile" than the consultant's role. The verdict is still out on the consultant change agent's role and its many advantages, which include the sponsorship of an institution, funds to operate, an agenda supported by a constituency (i.e., a university), etc., but some of its disadvantages are obvious. The institution might prevent the black consultant from functioning independently, or confine operations to the status quo, or permit only minimal "push," or cover too few issues related to change. For example, the Southern, white-dominated, bipartisan committee, which is always set up under progressive local governments as a means of resolving racial conflict, is analogous to the enervated black in a co-opted, consultant change agent's role. A bipartisan committee implies compromise, but compromise of basic rights and privileges, or of the actions required to right an aggrieved, longstanding condition, is insufficient.

Such roles as those labeled "human relations officer," etc., are generally reserved for blacks. *Thus the black in a white-dominated institution who seeks to initiate change experiences the psychological dilemma of being expected to push for change in the same style as that of the institution he or she is trying to change.* Frankly, it requires blacks to grit their teeth and be silent. Thus the role of the maverick is not only viable but necessary. The black maverick has the advantages of operating within the constraints (money, time, etc.) of a constituency—all is fair play—and retains his or her self-respect, although at high risk. The disadvantages are severe, however, since the maverick has no basis for confidence in his or her ability or style, and his or her motive and purposes are often questioned.

While these categories differ, their intent is similar; so it is important to know the differences.

Since institutional racism refers to those actions and behaviors by individuals which support such institutions, either knowingly or unknowingly, the constituency of the consultant in a change-agent role is worth mentioning. The student body of a university and its administration and faculty all become supporters of a human relations policy by virtue of their participation in the institution. They need not know of, or be involved in, the human relations activities to have constituency status. The burden, nevertheless, rests with them to dismiss and/or improve the human relations policy and programs, depending on their support or opposition.

The black, on the other hand, is on a collision course as soon as he or she is born. I recall a white woman's comment upon the birth of my twins: "Oh, they're so lovely; it's a shame that they must be brought into this world." Her meaning was clear, because the twins were black, and she meant well, but her words were ominous. Although our society professes moral support of minorities and cultural groups, it disdains them by its actions. It is against this background and in this context that the black change agent operates. This book, then, has been written for blacks and whites who wish to gain insight about the processes of generating change, but it has particular relevance for blacks. The black reader may better understand the different change-agent roles that blacks assume and the necessity for these roles. The black reader may also gain skills by using the model as it relates to the black consultant.

John Gardner, whose *Self-Renewal* (1965) cites evidence of the resistance of social institutions to change, calls for paying more attention to all our institutions. His thoughts, however, apply with particular accuracy to the problem of the black who seeks to generate change in a society that appears not to hear, let alone understand, the call for an end to institutional and individual racism. It becomes necessary to consider not just what changes are desired but the process by which change is accomplished. This is the charge to the black reader.

The personal risks, whether psychological or physical, for the black consultant (and any other generator of change) are not nearly as great as the risk of losing momentum in social programs, and it is for this reason that the model's stages will be emphasized. The stages represent clear-cut strategies that we believe are useful in all settings for persons who wish to follow the successive steps. Understandably, the ability and competence of the person who uses the model largely determines its utility; nevertheless, it is a logical framework from which to operate.

Stage I (Cultural and Racial Differences) is prerequisite to any deep understanding of race relations, and the black consultant plays a unique role in this stage. For example, the black is faced with whites (and even some blacks) who uncritically accept myths and stereotypes about blacks, such as, "Blacks are oversexed, lazy, and violent." Many such ignorant beliefs are held even today. After all, publishers and film studios began to produce realistic black themes only in the late 1960s, and the public is just beginning to gain some casual awareness of the problems of the black. But these problems are viewed with great concern *vis-à-vis* maintaining the white middle-class status quo. Proliferation of black themes is needed, but the impact is sudden and ungauged and often has the effect of "cornering" the viewers and readers, as opposed to broadening their concern for blacks and other cultural groups.

Generally speaking, these stereotypes were demeaning of blacks and caused their segregation by whites. Thus whites have created a vicious cycle of putting down blacks via stereotypes and then demeaning them behaviorally as a result—for example, making it impossible for blacks to get a decent education and then blaming them for being uneducated.

White participants need to share their feelings about blacks in a free and unprejudiced atmosphere; i.e., they must acknowledge that racial differences exist, determine what they mean, and label their own feelings about them—positive or negative. The myths and stereotypes have resulted in people uncritically internalizing attitudes toward blacks and other minority groups, and these attitudes, more often than not, have been negative. Thus the black consultant, in effect, is an encyclopedia of personal and impersonal experiences among blacks and whites. He or she handles questions unemotionally and uncritically in Stage I, whose importance is that of an introduction and an enticement, a positive reinforcer for serious involvement in the model.

The eventual outcome should be a white participant who is competent in setting pinpointed goals and measurable strategies to accomplish those goals over a given time period. The black consultant fills the need of whites to have a "black presence," because they might not otherwise be aware of the negative attitudes toward those who are unlike themselves or how they live. The fact is that a vast number of white citizenry are unaware of the plight and racial discrimination blacks experience. Although the model seeks to wean whites from the need for a black to help inform them, it is important that whites and blacks first learn about racial problems with the help of each other, before eventually acquiring independence and responsibility for their actions (or lack of action) toward minorities.

The black consultant in Stage I also plays the role of a

concerned listener, giving whites the opportunity—perhaps for the first time—to express all their biases and fears about interacting with blacks. Initially, they prefer to have the "private ear" of the black, because usually they are insecure about their attitudes and behavior toward blacks and may feel some guilt. They typically want to talk—and talk and talk—and the black consultant, patient and attentive, listens as they vent their feelings and concerns. Later, in Stage II (How Racism Operates) and particularly in Stage III (Examining Racial Attitudes), the "private ear" of the black consultant is turned off and the nonproductive comments of the whites are replaced by positive, affirmative-action comments. The likelihood of substantive comments by the white participants usually occurs in Stages IV (Sources of Racial Attitudes), V (Changing Behavior: What Can Be Done), and VI (Changing Behavior: How It Can Be Done).

Remember, the purpose of Stage I is to help participants become aware of their feelings and behavior toward minorities and to assume responsibility for them. In Stage I, therefore, it is appropriate to be helpful, to encourage discussion, and to be a good listener. The first stage, however, is not over until whites understand cultural differences and how they operate. Thus the goal of Stage I is that white participants understand their feelings about the differences between blacks and whites and be able to make personal judgments about them. Stage I might take a great deal of time to complete, but it is requisite for internalization of the points to be covered in the later stages of the model.

Stage II (How Racism Operates) is more academic and oriented to formal learning. The language is blunt, blame is placed, and a collision course develops. It administers a large dose of information and accountability. A prescribed time is set, which generally is too short for the white participants to accept all that they have heard. The white consultant plays an active role in Stage II because the intent is for the white consultant to assume blame and confess to involvement in the various forms of institutional and individual racism. The white consultant also attempts to define institutional and individual racism, cover historical points for emphasis, and discuss formal facts. Stage II does not expect whites and blacks (or other participants) to agree with the formal facts (although this is desired) but merely presents them. The black consultant "fills in" as the requirements of the participants seem to dictate, which usually means clarifying points and giving examples.

Both the black and the white consultants are teachers, in effect, in Stage II. The agenda is planned and the class (participants) is required to consider the formal material.

In *Stage III (Examining Racial Attitudes)* the black consultant takes on the critically active role of reinforcing racial attitudes and the results of the SAS. White participants are not "let off the hook" but are challenged to debate the meaning of their assessed racial attitudes. This stage is important because it represents the first challenge to their personal attitudes. The SAS is used as a group measure, but the white participants invariably defend their personal racial attitudes.

For example, whites often express dissatisfaction with negative attitudes toward blacks as measured by the SAS. In situation I (a black family moves next door), whites explain that "I don't mind if a black moves next door as long as he has the money to keep up his property." But were a white to move next door, the white neighbor would indicate a more positive feeling. It is the difference in attitudes toward a black and a white moving next door which is important, which the black consultant is often able to point out.

The reader should realize that it is strategically more important that the white consultant first present the SAS results and that the black consultant follow up by answering questions or clarifying interpretations; otherwise there is a real possibility that the black consultant, appearing to be "judge and jury" by presenting the SAS results of whites, might not get past explaining the nature of the instrument.

People are defensive about their racial attitudes and are unwilling participants. Thus it is important in Stage III that the black consultant not give the participants any cause to avoid discussion of the SAS results.

By the end of Stage III or by *Stage IV (Sources of Racial Attitudes),* the participants are ready to examine the sources of racial attitudes. They are more emotionally ready to critically examine the origins of racism and the institutions that support it. The black and the white consultants share a nondirective role. Generally, Stage IV is short, in comparison to the others.

Stage V (Changing Behavior: What Can Be Done) and *Stage VI (Changing Behavior: How It Can Be Done)* can be lengthy, but they often are shorter than Stage I. These later stages include developing goals and strategies, and again, the roles of the consultants may be nondirective. The black consultant assumes some explicit roles throughout the six stages of the model. He or she is positive, has a "take charge" quality, encourages talking, and does much reflecting in clarifying the participants' feelings in the initial stages. His or her attractiveness to the participants is generally high in the early stages, but this subsides to neutrality or even disdain in the later stages. The participants, exhorted to select goals and strategies, are made to feel that they are ultimately responsible for solving human relations problems.

The consultant role of the black can take a heavy toll of his or her mental and physical energy; therefore the role of the black in generating change requires serious preparation and a shrewd understanding of oneself. It is not an easy role, because of its double binds and abuse, but it is a very necessary role. Participants, in the end, may appreciate the black consultant's role, but their appreciation is not the criterion of success. *The criterion is the change that has occurred because of the involvement of the black consultant.*

9

The Unique Role Of The White

William E. Sedlacek

A white change agent or consultant provides many important and unique roles in developing procedures to eliminate racism. Generally, because the interplay between white and minority consultants serves as a role model for participants, a balance between the contributions of whites and minority persons should be maintained. That is, if one is conducting a workshop or conference, whites and minority people who make formal presentations or lead a given session should be alternated. Also, the schedule should be carefully constructed.

Our position is that there are *distinct* and *intentional* roles that change agents of different cultural and racial groups can and should play. Perhaps the best posture for any change agent is that of a goal-directed, nonemotional leader. The personal feelings and reactions of consultants should be set aside in the interest of accomplishing goals, but this is not to suggest that consultants should be artificial or unrealistic in their reactions. Rather, they should keep their eyes on long-range goals and should judge reactions in those terms. Will a reaction help or hurt the movement toward a goal? This is the question a good consultant must always keep in mind.

WHITE ROLES BY STAGE

Following is the stage-by-stage discussion of the unique roles a white consultant can play to bring about change.

Stage I (Cultural and Racial Differences) provides an important forum for the white consultant. Establishing rapport and credibility with those you are interested in changing is critical. We have conducted several workshops where this was not adequately done, and the results were poor in terms of moving through the model. "Credibility," for a white consultant, means being informed about racial and cultural differences and providing help and insight to others. The white consultant's role will often be secondary to a minority consultant in Stage I because the latter has been the target of racism and can relate his or her experiences and background to the points being made.

At the beginning, whites feel that they must hear it from the "horse's mouth" and thus listen eagerly to the minority consultants. It is important, then, that the white consultant be informed, helpful, and sensitive—but not to the point of feeling that he or she is interchangeable, so to speak, with a minority person. The white can never be an "insider" or a formal member of a minority group, because experience in the society precludes this: he or she cannot "think black." But it is important that a white demonstrate that it is possible to learn *about* racism through the experiences of others (with research) and by one's own observations. Indeed, this is the heart of the matter: one needn't belong to a minority group to understand racism. Without this premise, a model that focuses on white racism would be meaningless. In fact, it may be an advantage to be white, in understanding and combating racism, because only white individuals and institutions—by our definition—have the power to practice racism in America.

Thus a white consultant may have better entrée into these institutions than a minority person. This possibility should be used to full advantage at later points in the model.

Stage II (How Racism Operates) is important for the white consultant since it begins to deal with white people and institutions. It is often best to let the white consultant (or consultants) lead this session or stage because of the apparent validity of white knowledge of white institutions.

If the program is working properly, there is an early dependence on minorities to "tell it like it is," then a shift to the feeling that the white consultant has the "answer" to the ultimate responsibility for racism. The process is often gradual, but we feel the shift must be made or the model may not work. As noted earlier, the shift in dependency from the minority to the white consultant can be used as an intermediate criterion of success.

The white consultant should be able to answer hard questions put by a minority person, such as, "This is our issue and concern; what the hell do you know about it and why should you care?" A reasonable answer is that it *is* your issue (as a white) because it is whites who "set things up" and practice most of the racism, which has made you what you are. You don't like it, and it is your responsibility to change it. Many minority people may still be skeptical, but your job is to convince them through your actions.

You can expect many minority people to demand and challenge your motive. If you are able to state a reasonable motive (such as that noted above) and back it up with *behavior,* many people will at least give you benefit of the doubt.

Another question, this time from whites, that a white change agent should be able to answer is, "What makes you

so superior to the rest of us? Aren't you a racist too?" A possible answer is that you are *not* superior but simply a racist
who has learned about racism and is trying to do something
about it.

Straightforward, unemotional, analytical responses are
recommended. Honesty and behavior that is consistent with
one's stated values breed credibility.

Stage III (Examining Racial Attitudes) is most critical,
thus far, for the white consultant. The topic is emotional and
difficult to handle. Having a white consultant introduce and
discuss the SAS is the best procedure because people are better
able to disagree or argue with a white person. The white consultant should remain calm, unemotional, and analytical, and
should continue to bring participants back to the goals. After
the white consultant has handled this stage, it is often best
for the black or minority consultant to "wrap it up" and
reinforce the goals of the stage.

If a black initially covers the SAS results, the participants may not be able either to generate or vent strong reactions. If this occurs, it may be difficult or impossible to move
them further in the model. Getting things "off their chests"
with the white consultant makes them ready to hear what the
black consultant has to say.

It is difficult for one consultant (or all-black or all-white
consultants) to carry the full load throughout the model.
Black (or minority) and white consultants are critically
needed at various points. For instance, a white would have
difficulty handling Stage I alone because of a lack of knowledge or credibility. In turn, many blacks have difficulty dealing with white racial attitudes.

Ultimately, our concern must be with what moves people
through the model, rather than the needs and abilities of the
consultants. Consultants or change agents should be optimally
employed.

Stage IV (Sources of Racial Attitudes) emphasizes moving from the emotional aspects of racial attitudes toward a less emotional analysis and understanding the sources and consequences of racial attitudes. Here white and minority consultants play similar roles, with emphasis on getting the participants to help themselves. Any emotional spillover from Stage III, however, is probably best handled by the white consultant.

In *Stages V and VI (Goals and Strategies)* the white and the black consultants again play similar roles in having the participants assume the responsibility for action. The consultants should be less direct or "in charge" than they may have been earlier and should interject questions as to whether the accomplishment of a particular goal will work against racism or whether a particular strategy is feasible. Serving as "resources" who state goals and comment on the experience and strategies of others is an important role for black and white consultants. But the main creative work in Stages V and VI should come from the participants.

GENERAL ADVICE FOR WHITES IN RACE RELATIONS

The role of the white consultant or change agent in relation to the model was explored above, but there is general advice that is applicable to any white person who is contemplating or is already engaged in race relations work. The first principle is *integrity*—that is, an honest, straightforward approach. Most minority people have had to develop keen antennae for understanding whites, so as to survive, but it has mattered little to most whites whether or not they understood minorities. Recognizing that you, as a white, are a racist and have contributed to racism is one way of showing your integrity.

Don't be a "great white buddy," or a gushing, bleeding-heart liberal, but simply a straightforward, honest person who knows something about what is going on and is sincerely trying to come to grips with racism. This is critical in establishing a good relationship with a minority person. You will make mistakes, but your honesty and integrity will come through; and if you learn from your mistakes, minority people will begin to respect you.

Having said all this, we must caution the well-intentioned white against becoming a doormat and being exploited by minority people. Many individuals taunt and "lean on" whites to see whether there is anything real in their supposed enlightenment. I have seen more than one "put on" of this kind, and Alinsky (1971) gives us a good example of this. He reports being asked to assist some Canadian Indians in organizing:

> The conversation began with my suggesting that the general approach should be that the Indians get together, crossing all tribal lines, and organize. Because of their relatively small numbers I thought that they should then work with various sectors of the white liberal population, gain them as allies, and then begin to move nationally. Immediately I ran into the rationalizations. The dialogue went something like this (I should preface this by noting that it was quite obvious what was happening since I could see from the way the Indians were looking at each other they were thinking: "So we invite this white organizer from south of the border to come up here and he tells us to get organized and to do these things. What must be going through his mind is: 'What's wrong with you Indians that you have been sitting around here for a couple of hundred years now and you haven't organized to do these things?' " And so it began):

INDIANS:
>   Well, we can't organize.

ME:

Why not?

INDIANS:

Because that's a white man's way of doing things.

ME:

(I decided to let that one pass though it obviously was untrue, since mankind from time immemorial has always organized, regardless of what race or color they were, whenever they wanted to bring about change): I don't understand.

INDIANS:

Well, you see, if we organize, that means getting out and fighting the way you are telling us to do and that would mean that we would be corrupted by the white man's culture and lose our own values.

ME:

What are these values that you would lose?

INDIANS:

Well, there are all kinds of values.

ME:

Like what?

INDIANS:

Well, there's creative fishing.

ME:

What do you mean, creative fishing?

INDIANS:

Creative fishing.

ME:

I heard you the first time. What is this creative fishing?

INDIANS:

Well, you see, when you whites go out and fish, you just go out and fish, don't you?

ME:

Yeah, I guess so.

INDIANS:

> Well, you see, when we go out and fish, we fish creatively.

ME:

> Yeah. That's the third time you've come around with that. What is this creative fishing?

INDIANS:

> Well, to begin with, when we go out fishing, we get away from everything. We get way out in the woods.

ME:

> Well, we whites don't exactly go fishing in Times Square, you know.

INDIANS:

> Yes, but it's different with us. When we go out, we're out on the water and you can hear the lap of the waves on the bottom of the canoe, and the birds in the trees and the leaves rustling, and—you know what I mean?

ME:

> No, I don't know what you mean. Furthermore, I think that that's just a pile of shit. Do you believe it yourself?

> This brought a shocked silence. It should be noted that I was not being profane purely for the sake of being profane, I was doing this purposefully. If I had responded in a tactful way, saying, "Well, I don't quite understand what you mean," we would have been off for a ride around the rhetorical ranch for the next thirty days. Here profanity became literally an up-against-the-wall bulldozer [pp. 110–112].

Alinsky further noted that the National Film Board of Canada had shot this scene for a documentary. When the film was shown to a meeting of white Canadian social workers and Indians, the whites were shocked and embarrassed and looked at the floor or glanced sideways at the Indians. When the film was over, an Indian stood up and said: "When Mr. Alinsky told us we were full of shit, that was the first time a white man has really talked to us as equals—you would never say that to us. You would always say 'Well, I can see your point of view but I'm a little confused' and stuff like that. In other words you treat us as children" (p. 122).

The Indians may not have been trying to put Alinsky on but they respected him for his refusal to pretend he understood them.

We feel, however, that whites must also understand how they are different from minority people—the similarities will take care of themselves. In other words, we must have both an intellectual and an emotional understanding of another's point of view to expect a realistic relationship to develop. There are many differences among subgroups, but the following are some general points that, though applicable to other minorities, focus on blacks.

Blacks, who have grown up with prejudice and racism, deal with it every day of their lives in one way or another. Indeed, many blacks are so used to it that they may no longer notice it, or they may not think of it as out of the ordinary. But few, if any, whites in the United States have had such experiences. I have on occasion been the only white at a meeting or event, and nothing very negative happened to me on those occasions, but if it had, I know I could step outside and be back in my own environment as I routinely went through my daily life. This is not the case for blacks.

The daily routine for the typical black requires that he or she interact with *"Mister* Charlie" or *"Miss* Ann," for they are the ones with power. Thus even if a white receives discrimination and "hassling" because of his or her race, it will be limited to the short term. A black experiences it day in and day out; and there is no way to share such an experience with a white. The white who understands this has a chance to form a good relationship with a black.

Some might argue, "Well, a middle-class or well-to-do black doesn't have the same experiences as a lower-class black." To some extent this is true, but discrimination against the former takes different forms. Just a few examples will illustrate this: blacks are checked more closely than whites when cashing a check; blacks have greater problems finding a physician and a hospital that will provide good care and treat them with dignity; blacks must consider many physical and psychological implications in deciding whether to buy a house in an all-white neighborhood; and blacks must think twice before they park on the street when attending, say, a meeting in a white neighborhood, because they might be stopped by the police. The list could go on and on. Few whites have ever had such treatment.

Throughout this book we have been making the point that whites should be responsible for their racism, and a personal example may help us understand the point. My wife and I were in Chicago between planes, and because our parents lived in the area, we arranged to have dinner with them at the best restaurant at O'Hare Field. The customary behavior in such a group is to discuss pleasant, noncontroversial topics, but the inevitable question was asked: What was I doing? When I described some of my activities, my parents were surprised and did not understand. I could have lied, or talked about something else, but I had already decided to deal with racism whenever it occurred. Questions about "colored" people were asked—why they wear "outrageous" clothes— and we were told how property values go down when the "colored" move in, etc., which I attempted to counter with facts.

Eventually my parents said: "Well, we might do something about racism but we don't know any 'colored' people so there isn't much we can do." I then said that, if they were serious, they could begin by not using "colored," and I went into a brief explanation of why. My parents responded with "Well, we don't mean anything bad by the word; that's just the way we were brought up. They should just understand and get used to it." To make my father understand what his use of the word implied, I casually called him a "motherfucker." After he and the others had recovered from the shock they realized that it doesn't matter if a word means nothing in particular to the user; what counts is its effect on the person to whom it is applied.

There are several important principles involved here. First, whites should *seek* occasions to deal with racism; failure to do so aggravates the problem. My particular strategy was effective with my parents, who now use "black" instead of "colored" and have some idea of the issues involved in racism.

Second, I think my deliberate boorishness provided a chance for a white to get a glimpse of what it might be like to be black. (But please keep in mind my earlier comments on the difference between day-in day-out and occasional discrimination.) Such strategies don't always work, and I have bungled opportunities, or handled them badly, on more than one occasion; but if you follow the tenets of the model and modify your strategies as you learn, you will improve.

Third, it helps drive home the point we have tried to make so often: whites are responsible for their racism, and they can take action, however minor, to change it—even if they have never seen a black. If whites would use their communication skills in dealing with racism, it would be obvious to them that "colored" is an insulting word.

The last major point is *persistence,* since most whites expect too much too soon from blacks or other minority people. How often have you heard, "Well, I tried; I invited them to join but they said no"? Nonsense! Most blacks have had a lifetime of negative experiences with whites; why, then, should they believe it would be different on this or that occasion? It may take hundreds and hundreds of honest and positive overtures from whites to alter the behavior pattern of even a single black toward whites.

So hang in there, make the attempt because it is the right thing to do, not because of any immediate reinforcement you may want. In fact, any white who does antiracism work, either at a formal or informal level, will be viewed with skepticism and suspicion by many. Minority people may resent your "intrusion," and whites are suspicious of one of their own who "turns" on them. Again, the good change agent has forceful answers, is often a "loner," and is positively reinforced by change, not by the comments of others.

A quote from *Pogo* may best end this chapter: "We have met the enemy, and they is us."

10

Evaluation
And Final
Comments

Throughout this book we have stressed the need for evaluation or assessing progress in social change efforts; now we turn to evaluating the model itself: How do we know it works? We have also stressed that each stage includes certain objectives, whose accomplishment constitutes a positive outcome for that stage. For instance, if participants understand that cultural and racial differences exist, Stage I has been at least partially successful. This can be discerned by discussions during which participants are "tested" on their understanding of this point, or one can be more formal and give a written quiz at the end of Stage I.

In Chapter 6, we discussed a four-part evaluation scheme: information, attitude change, outcome goals, and additional objective evidence. These fit the development of the model rather directly. In Stages I and II, and perhaps IV, information is the principal criterion. Do participants know that cultural and racial differences exist? Do they understand institutional racism? Do they understand the sources of their racial attitudes?

Stage III directly concerns attitude change. The SAS could be used as a before-and-after measure of this stage, but often the point is made with the SAS and verbal reports of understanding are used for evaluation. Chapman (1974) used questionnaires that assess the behavioral intentions of college-student groups to do work relating to racism as evidence of the success of Stage II (How Racism Operates) and the SAS to assess readiness to approach Stage III (Examining Racial Attitudes).

The third type of evaluation, outcome goals, is the emphasis of the whole model and the specific goal of Stages V and VI. If clear goals are stated in Stage V, that stage has been successful. And if strategies are developed in Stage VI, it too has been successful. You must determine whether the goals are accomplished, which can be difficult to assess for several reasons. First, long-term goals take time to implement. Second, periodic follow-ups should be made on specific goals and strategies.

As of this writing, approximately 60 percent of the goals we have stated have been accomplished, at least in part. We currently have a study under way to determine this figure more exactly and to identify the reasons for lack of accomplishment.

A third difficulty is identifying the "spinoff" effects of a given strategy. For instance, after we accomplished our goal of developing a black parent advisory group in a secondary school, this group became a catalyst for the accomplishment of many other goals relating to racism. Thus, although we accomplished only one goal, its effects were far reaching. Quality, then, can be more critical than quantity. The accomplishment of only one critical goal can turn a school around. And again, it is the accomplishment of the goal that is important, not who gets credit for it.

The fourth type of evaluation—additional objective evidence—is almost a strategy for evaluating others. For instance, in evaluating a program that is run by someone else, it is feasible to allow the presentation of objective evidence that was not included in the other types of evaluation. This might reduce the complaint that the evaluation procedure excludes pertinent evidence. As we noted in Chapter 6, we feel all evaluations can be placed in the first three types.

Hedman (1975), who studied an overall evaluation of our model in an experimental study, compared two versions of the model (with student teachers at the university level) to a control group. One version represented discussion and interaction, as described in this book, and the other involved an edited version of an audiotape (Sedlacek, 1974) and limited discussion. Hedman found no differences between the experimental and control groups: both groups interacted negatively with black students.

Troy, Sedlacek, and Chapman (1975), who demonstrated the efficacy of the model with university freshmen in orientation programs, found that the students were able to work through the model and devise goals and strategies that they could use as students on campus.

Obviously, many more evaluations should be developed for the model and its components, but thus far the evidence for its validity as a strategy for eliminating racism looks promising.

OTHER MINORITIES AND OTHER GROUPS

We have presented the model as applying to all cultural-racial groups, but we have noted that most of our general data and specific experiences have been in black-white situations.

The model would seem to generalize quite readily for any cultural-racial minority in the United States, and very likely in other countries as well. All "outgroups," in the power sense, suffer from some form of institutionalized discrimination, and the research on attitudes (described in Stage III) showed that majority groups tend to generalize their feelings toward culturally relevant outgroups.

Additionally, our definition of racism, also developed in Stage III, includes discrimination against any group which is identifiable and thereby receives negative outcomes. Not all of these groups are racial; most of them, according to our definition, probably are cultural. That is, the people in these groups share common characteristics or behavior. In most of our applications, we broaden the concept of racism to encompass many groups and make our points where we can.

We are reminded of the criticism we received from a university administrator who felt our approach was not "intellectual" because it did not deal specifically with Nazi Germany, the most relevant form of racism he had encountered in his sixty-year life. Our counterargument was that we were trying to teach by using examples from the immediate environment of the participants. If, in their experience, the most common form of racism was against blacks, this form should be used to demonstrate the process. To emphasize Nazi Germany would have made the topic more academic and historical, and thus less relevant.

If we do our job well, we can generalize racism to other times and circumstances. However, one should determine what form of racism would best make the point.

We want people to work on their immediate environment rather than be content with understanding a problem as if it were far removed. The model forces us to examine racism, as it exists, wherever we are. Hopefully, this will give timelessness to the model, and if we find ourselves dealing with as-yet-unidentified minorities in the future, we need not start from scratch to develop new change models.

A dramatic example of reactions to outgroups occurred in a class on racism, taught by the senior author, when he brought the president of the Student Homophile Association to discuss the work his group was doing and the reasons for its existence. At first the class participants, who were mostly teachers, were repulsed by the speaker and his topic, but they were not afraid to voice their negative feelings toward homosexuals. However, these same people would be loath to admit any negative feelings toward blacks. I used this point to help them understand that public rejection of homosexuals corresponds to the situation *vis-à-vis* blacks forty years ago. Whether each minority group moves through the same process in gaining public understanding and acceptance is hard to say, but it appears that individuals are influenced by peer norms as to proper feelings and behavior toward such groups (Sedlacek and Brooks, 1971a). This point must be considered in applying the model to a group such as homosexuals, and longer periods of time may be needed in certain stages, especially Stage I.

WOMEN AND SEXISM

One topic that is receiving increased attention is sexism, which is another specific form of racism. That women are operationally discriminated against is clear at every level of our society, and nearly every issue we have raised in this book also applies to women, who are a specific cultural group, according to our definition. Weisstein (1971) suggests that women are characterized in our culture as "inconsistent, emotionally unstable, lacking in a strong conscience or superego, weaker, 'nurturant' rather than productive, 'intuitive' rather than intelligent and, if they are at all 'normal,' suited to the home and family . . . and if they know their place, which is in the home, they are really quite lovable, happy, childlike, loving creatures" (p. 372).

Of course, young girls are socialized into fulfilling these roles, and, as with any cultural group, the point where stereotypes end and true cultural differences begin becomes blurred. One reason why we know so little about individual differences among women is that we have done very little research on female subjects. A report by the Task Force on the Status of Women in Psychology of the American Psychological Association found that women are almost "invisible" in frequently used psychology texts (Birk et al., 1974). It concluded that not only was the language biased toward the masculine (*he, him*) but that few studies or examples concentrated on women. Several strategies we have employed in countering these problems are to use nonsexist reference words (e.g., *him or her*), to do research involving women subjects and sexism, and to insist that students who work on theses and dissertations address these issues directly when selecting subjects for a paper.

Our studies have developed a number of interesting findings related to sexism and women's issues. Herman and Sedlacek (1974a) found that women who major in education are more likely to follow traditional expectations of the relationship between a career and a family than women who major in the physical sciences. The former, that is, are more willing to forgo a career for a home and family. Herman and Sedlacek (1973b) also found that most university students favor adoption of a curriculum in women's studies and are most interested in a course on the sociology of women. In a study on female university student and staff perceptions of rape, Herman and Sedlacek (1974b) found that about half the women sampled were eager to have the topic discussed and to have preventive programs developed, while the other half were afraid to deal with it. Most women, however, felt that the university was not doing enough to prevent rape on the campus.

Attitudes relating to sexism were explored in several other studies. Collins and Sedlacek (1974) found that female students who enter a university counseling center are more likely to be labeled as having social or emotional problems than males, who were more often seen as having vocational or educational problems. Clients were also more apt to attend a first appointment-interview with a male counselor than with a female counselor.

Whether females actually have more social or emotional problems, or are more likely to be labeled as having them, is not clear. However, J. L. Gardner (1971) states (p. 713) that "therapy is bad for women. Right now in our excessively sexist society, it is unlikely that *anyone,* without special training in feminism, can create conditions which would encourage females to 'exercise their right to select goals if these goals are at variance with the goals of the counselor.' The goals of counselors trained in traditional programs can hardly be expected to do other than reflect the sexist values."

Faculty attitudes toward blacks, females, and undergraduates in general were compared, and it was found that the faculty had overly positive stereotypes of blacks and females and wished to avoid expressing attitudes toward these groups (Christensen and Sedlacek, 1974). In other words, they wished to think of blacks and women in an idealized way rather than consider them as real people. Thus the faculty was generally at Stage I of the model in that they did not want to deal with realistic differences among their students.

This again demonstrated the problems in assessing attitudes toward cultural and racial groups; so a version of the SAS, aimed at sexism, was developed (see Exhibit 2).

EXHIBIT 2

This questionnaire measures how people think and feel about a number of social and personal incidents and situations. It is not a test, so there are no right or wrong answers. The questionnaire is anonymous, so please *do not sign your name.*

Each item or situation is followed by 10 descriptive word scales. Your task is to select, for each descriptive scale, the rating which best describes *your* feelings toward the item.

Sample item: Going out on a date

happy | A | B | C | D | E | sad

You would indicate the direction and extent of your feelings; e.g., you might select (B) by indicating your choice, (B), on your response sheet by blackening the appropriate space for that word scale. *Do not mark the booklet. Please respond to all word scales.*

Sometimes you may feel as though you had the same item before on the questionnaire. This will not be the case, so *do not look back and forth* through the items. Do not try to remember how you checked similar items earlier in the questionnaire. *Make each item a separate and independent judgment.* Respond as honestly as possible without puzzling over individual items. Respond with your first impressions whenever possible.

SITUATIONS

Form A

I. It is evening and a person appears at your door selling magazines.

II. You are stopped for speeding by a police officer.

III. You have just met your new doctor.

IV. You have just learned that you have been fired and a co-worker takes over your job.

V. You meet the person who will complete your income tax return.

VI. You pull into a service station and the attendant looks under the car hood.

VII. You are in a hospital and the nurse comes in to give you an injection.

VIII. You go out for a drink with a friend who decides to pick up the check.

IX. You are a personnel officer and have just interviewed an applicant who appears to be aggressive and bright.

X. You come to the Counseling Center and meet your counselor for the first time.

Form B

I. It is evening and a woman appears at your door selling magazines.

II. You are stopped for speeding by a policewoman.

III. You have just met your new woman doctor.

IV. You have just learned that you have been fired and a female co-worker takes over your job.

V. You meet the woman who will complete your income tax return.

VI. You pull into a service station and the female attendant looks under the car hood.

VII. You are in a hospital and the male nurse comes in to give you an injection.

VIII. You go out for a drink with a girl friend who decides to pick up the check.

IX. You are a personnel officer and have just interviewed a woman applicant who appears to be aggressive and bright.

X. You come to the Counseling Center and meet your female counselor for the first time.

Called the Situational Attitude Scale for Women (SAS-W), it depicts women in nontraditional roles in form B. Form A is neutral. In one situation, a male nurse is depicted in form B. Herman and Sedlacek (1973a) found consistent differences in how men respond to each form, which can be taken as evidence that the references to women in form B caused the subjects to respond differently than they did in form A (see Table 3).

A closer examination of the statistical analysis reveals some interesting patterns. While the situations generally varied greatly in how much they differentiated between the questionnaire forms, two were quite consistent: the woman selling magazines and the woman service station attendant. Less con-

TABLE 3
Means, Standard Deviations, and *t* Tests for Forms A and B*
of the SAS–W

Item	Situations†	Form A (N = 51) Mean	SD	Form B (N = 59) Mean	SD	t‡
	I. Woman Selling Magazines					
1	Relaxed–startled	1.63	1.10	1.37	1.06	1.22
2	Receptive–cautious	2.57	0.95	1.71	1.18	4.11
3	Excited–unexcited	3.06	0.96	2.54	1.17	2.49
4	Glad–angered	2.29	0.64	1.86	0.65	3.46
5	Pleased–annoyed	2.59	0.91	2.05	0.79	3.28
6	Indifferent–suspicious	1.80	1.07	1.66	1.19	0.65
7	Tolerable–intolerable	1.53	0.98	1.03	0.90	2.74
8	Afraid–secure	2.78	0.99	3.07	0.95	1.53
9	Friend–enemy	1.90	0.72	1.37	0.76	3.70
10	Unprotected–protected	2.61	1.07	2.83	1.11	1.06
	II. Policewoman					
11	Calm–nervous	3.35	0.76	2.64	1.19	3.62
12	Trusting–suspicious	2.25	1.08	2.08	1.20	0.77
13	Afraid–safe	1.47	0.98	1.83	1.11	1.78
14	Friendly–unfriendly	1.29	1.35	1.12	1.04	0.76
15	Tolerant–intolerant	1.10	1.29	0.98	0.95	0.53
16	Bitter–pleasant	2.08	1.38	2.27	1.22	0.77
17	Cooperative–uncooperative	0.51	0.87	0.39	0.74	0.78
18	Acceptive–belligerent	1.22	1.05	1.14	0.95	0.42
19	Inferior–superior	1.78	0.94	1.97	0.88	1.04
20	Serious–humorous	0.80	1.12	1.19	1.11	1.78
	III. Woman Doctor					
21	Apprehensive–confident	1.71	1.11	1.66	1.22	0.20
22	Nervous–calm	1.98	1.20	1.71	1.09	1.22
23	Angry–jovial	2.63	0.79	2.44	0.89	1.15
24	Unsure–sure	1.96	0.88	1.76	1.20	0.96
25	Slighted–understanding	2.47	0.87	2.75	1.02	1.50
26	Embarrassed–not embarrassed	2.96	1.08	2.19	1.13	3.62
27	Confident–not confident	1.53	0.96	1.63	0.99	0.52

TABLE 3 (Continued)

Item	Situations†	Form A (N = 51) Mean	SD	Form B (N = 59) Mean	SD	t‡
28	Aroused–passive	2.20	0.93	1.80	1.00	2.13
29	Disappointed–elated	2.10	0.45	2.20	0.82	0.81
30	Threatened–neutral	3.33	0.83	3.05	1.03	1.55
IV.	Female Co-worker					
31	Resentful–tolerant	1.00	1.12	1.37	1.12	1.73
32	Unjustified–justified	0.94	0.75	1.54	1.06	3.34
33	Disgusted–pleased	0.67	0.81	1.15	0.86	3.01
34	Incensed–cautious	1.69	0.96	1.95	1.02	1.38
35	Angry–calm	0.90	0.80	1.20	1.04	1.67
36	Unreasonable–reasonable	1.75	1.20	1.90	1.12	0.67
37	Going too far–fair	1.45	1.00	1.81	1.20	1.69
38	Acceptable–objectionable	2.80	0.97	2.27	1.19	2.52
39	Furious–accepting	1.50	0.98	1.80	1.07	1.48
40	Wrong–right	1.45	1.05	1.71	0.95	1.32
V.	Woman Completing Income Tax					
41	Irritated–calm	2.88	0.90	2.86	1.19	0.09
42	Skeptical–assured	2.18	1.02	2.59	1.28	1.85
43	Incredible–credible	2.59	0.69	2.83	1.03	1.41
44	Useful–useless	1.37	1.15	1.24	1.15	0.61
45	Competent–incompetent	1.16	0.92	1.08	1.03	0.38
46	Ridiculous–expected	2.51	0.87	2.43	0.87	0.47
47	Cheated–fulfilled	2.47	0.78	2.59	0.95	0.68
48	Trusting–lack of trust	1.39	0.97	1.48	1.15	0.44
49	Inadequate–adequate	2.53	0.94	2.71	1.07	0.91
50	Humorous–furious	2.65	1.01	2.21	1.19	2.06
VI.	Female Service Station Attendant					
51	Furious–pleased	3.14	1.07	2.53	1.25	2.71
52	Apprehensive–confident	2.41	1.19	1.83	1.30	2.40
53	Surprised–expected	2.02	1.24	0.90	1.10	4.97
54	Funny–not funny	2.45	1.07	1.42	1.14	4.80
55	Confidence–lack of confidence	1.51	1.24	2.00	1.07	6.26
56	Silly–proper	3.02	1.04	1.75	1.07	6.26

TABLE 3 (Continued)

Item	Situations†	Form A (N = 51) Mean	SD	Form B (N = 59) Mean	SD	t‡
57	Superior–inferior	1.67	0.90	1.93	0.99	1.45
58	Excited–not excited	2.60	1.06	2.08	1.18	2.36
59	Improper–proper	3.10	1.03	2.03	1.12	5.10
60	Feminine–masculine	2.98	0.96	2.42	1.21	2.62
	VII. Male Nurse					
61	Surprised–expected	2.22	1.32	1.98	1.33	0.91
62	Feminine–masculine	2.20	1.28	2.44	1.11	1.06
63	Slow–quick	2.31	1.15	2.12	0.90	0.99
64	Dumb–smart	2.40	0.98	2.44	1.06	0.20
65	Out of place–in place	2.33	1.29	2.36	1.23	0.12
66	Oddball–normal	2.63	1.17	2.53	1.21	0.44
67	Distasteful–tasteful	2.12	1.08	2.32	1.17	0.94
68	Proper–improper	1.10	0.98	1.59	1.19	2.34
69	Good–bad	1.67	1.23	1.39	1.07	1.25
70	Annoyed–pleased	1.71	1.24	1.90	1.07	0.87
	VIII. Girl Friend Picks Up Check					
71	Embarrased–relaxed	2.31	1.11	1.97	1.34	1.45
72	Uncomfortable–comfortable	2.33	1.13	2.02	1.31	1.33
73	Unsure–confident	2.59	1.01	1.95	1.29	2.82
74	Unexpected–expected	1.08	0.95	1.10	1.16	0.11
75	Put down–not put down	2.94	1.00	2.56	1.23	1.76
76	Hurt–not hurt	2.82	1.10	2.56	1.31	1.13
77	Annoyed–pleased	2.78	0.94	2.32	1.33	2.05
78	Disappointed–satisfied	2.75	0.90	2.44	1.20	1.47
79	Distasteful–tasteful	2.49	0.92	2.34	1.20	0.70
80	Feminine–masculine	2.90	1.05	2.37	1.27	2.33
	IX. Woman Job Applicant					
81	Good–bad	0.57	0.82	0.80	1.05	1.24
82	Surprised–not surprised	1.75	1.04	2.36	1.29	2.68
83	Threatening–non-threatening	2.57	0.95	2.76	1.23	0.91
84	Unpleasant–pleasant	3.00	0.89	3.03	0.95	0.19
85	Provocative–undesirable	1.39	0.93	1.19	1.02	1.09

TABLE 3 (Continued)

Item	Situations†	Form A (N = 51) Mean	SD	Form B (N = 59) Mean	SD	t‡
86	Unattractive–attractive	2.45	1.05	2.69	1.12	1.16
87	Domineering–outgoing	2.69	0.98	2.53	1.08	0.81
88	Problem–asset	2.82	1.08	2.81	1.02	0.05
89	Masculine–feminine	0.96	0.93	2.17	1.24	5.67
90	Exciting–unexciting	1.64	0.93	1.20	0.84	2.55
	X. Female Counselor					
91	Mothered–independent	2.41	1.11	2.20	1.15	0.96
92	Gypped–good deal	2.39	1.03	2.27	0.92	0.65
93	Uncomfortable–comfortable	1.88	1.17	2.51	1.10	2.88
94	Aroused–unaroused	2.02	0.94	2.07	0.99	0.26
95	Nervous–calm	1.92	1.22	2.47	1.09	2.48
96	Disappointed–elated	2.18	0.76	2.31	0.72	0.90
97	Guarded–open	2.25	1.19	2.47	1.01	1.04
98	Humorous–serious	2.28	1.28	1.92	1.09	1.59
99	Out of place–in place	2.51	1.16	2.54	1.09	0.15
100	Masculine–feminine	1.10	093	2.15	1.22	4.99

*Scale A to E (numerical equivalent, 0 to 4).
†See Exhibit 2 p. 166 for complete situation.
‡All t values larger than 1.98 are significant beyond .05 (2-tailed test).

sistent, but nonetheless showing differentiation between the forms, were the items where women were counselors, aggressive job applicants, co-workers taking over another's job, and girl friends picking up the check.

However, the most interesting finding was that attitudes in many of these situations were more positive toward women than to an individual whose sex was unspecified (usually assumed to be a man). Encountering a magazine salesperson, men were found to feel more angered and annoyed than when they encountered a magazine saleswoman. They also felt more cautious toward the male, considered the situation more in-

tolerable, and tended to think of the salesman as an enemy.
They were also more excited about the prospect of a saleswoman. It is possible that what was tapped here is a more or
less realistic appraisal of the danger of violence when a male
is seen at the door after nightfall, as opposed to seeing a
female. This, however, is a stereotyped response as not all
males are capable of more violence than females nor are all
females nonviolent.

Likewise, when males admitted they felt more nervous
being stopped by a police officer than by a policewoman, this
may have indicated the belief that men are more likely to
hold power than women. Again, the assumption is that the
person in the neutral, form A situation is thought of as a male.
While this is not necessarily a negative attitude toward men
or women, it is nonetheless a stereotyped belief. Again, in the
situation where men were seen by a woman doctor, they felt
more embarrassed and more aroused than if they had been
visiting a doctor whose sex was unspecified. This indicates
that men did not see the doctor only as a professional but also
as a woman. Seeing a woman working as an income tax consultant was considered humorous.

The situation that aroused the most negative feelings
toward women was the one in which the service station attendant was a female. Men were furious to find a woman; or
they lacked confidence and found the situation funny, unexpected, and silly. Nonetheless, the attendant was perceived as
feminine and exciting. This situation reflects the generalized
(and often erroneous) belief that women have "no head" for
mechanics, as well as the fact that a woman is seen as a sex
object in any situation.

Another situation that caused discomfort in the male
subjects was a girl friend's picking up the check. The men felt
unsure and annoyed, and felt that paying the check was a
masculine thing to do. When a woman applicant for a job

was described as bright and aggressive, the subjects were not surprised, and chose "feminine" and "exciting" to describe their reactions. Their lack of surprise could have been due to increased male awareness of the women's liberation movement and its connotations.

Situations that were viewed more favorably when women were involved included the woman counselor. Men, on the whole, seemed to be more comfortable and calmer with a female counselor. It must be remembered that counseling and psychology have traditionally been receptive to female participation and are seen as an extension of woman's nurturant role in society (Adams, 1971). Again, this seems to confirm a stereotyped view of woman's ability.

One item did not fit this general pattern. When a female co-worker was depicted as taking another employee's job, less disgust and fewer objections were recorded than when the sex of the co-worker was not noted (form A). Respondents believed the former situation was more justified than the latter.

Since the object of the study was the attitudes of males toward females, the responses of females were analyzed separately. Females responded more positively to form B for all situations except the service station attendant, choosing "surprised," "lack of confidence," and "excited" to express their feelings toward a female service station attendant. Their response was most positive to a new female doctor: more confident, calm, sure, or neutral. Thus females seemed to hold liberated attitudes in commonly expected situations, but still found a female service station attendant incongruous. It should be recalled that the sample was small (forty-one) and that the SAS–W contains situations designed to create a response in males rather than females; whether it is equally relevant for females is an open question. A controlled study, employing equal numbers of males and females in a two-way analysis of variance design, would seem to be called for.

Although responses to the two forms did not immediately appear to measure sexism, a closer examination disclosed that sexism appears to be more than a negative reaction. More exactly, it is a stereotyped reaction to any change in the roles for either sex. The scale in that respect would seem to be a valuable tool for measuring an elusive and complex attitude. However, more studies must be done to check the consistency and generalizability of the results. Additionally, studies exploring new contexts and situations should be conducted. For instance, Spence and Helmreich (1972) found three factors in the attitudes of males toward females: masculine superiority, equality of opportunity for women, and social and sexual relationships. While the SAS–W appears to contain situations relevant to each of these factors, it may prove fruitful to construct new situations around them. Also, we have a number of other studies under way on the SAS–W. Thus while we need more experience in applying the model to women, there appears to be more and more material on sexism that makes application of the model all the more direct.

Chapman (1974) conducted an experiment using the SAS and the SAS–W and a measure of interest in financial support for activities for blacks and women as criteria. Using the Starpower simulation game, he randomly assigned white freshmen and transfer students at a university to one of four groups that would receive the following experiences: (1) Starpower and racism discussion only, (2) Starpower and sexism discussion only, (3) Starpower and racism and sexism discussion, and (4) a control group which played an unrelated game called Meet the Bureaucracy, with no racism or sexism discussion. (Starpower is a game in which the participants bargain and trade chips according to rules that create a three-tier society of "haves," "have-nots," and a middle class. This is supposed to simulate the feelings of members of a certain social class.)

Chapman defined racism as applying to racial or ethnic-related groups only, while sexism concerns attitudes and behavior toward women. He found that the experimental groups (1, 2, and 3) had significantly more favorable attitudes or behavior toward blacks and/or females than did the control group on all the criterion measures. However, he also found that the group that discussed racism *and* sexism (group 3) showed more positive attitudes and behavior toward blacks and women than either group that discussed racism or sexism only.

While many explanations for his results are possible, there are several that appear to be particularly plausible. First, by presenting examples of both racism and sexism, one has a greater range of material with which to demonstrate or make the key points in the model. A second and related explanation is that one can reach a particular individual better with either a racism or a sexism argument, which in turn helps him or her see the relationship to all minorities. For instance, if a white women has little feeling for what racism against blacks is like, relating it to her experiences as a woman may help her understand it. (Chapman's study also demonstrates that it is possible to do experimental field research in an area where the little research that has been done to date has tended to be of the descriptive survey type.)

The relationship between racism and sexism is never more complicated than when it pertains to black women. We have discussed this relationship at several points in the book, but we remind you that there is an interaction between race and sex. As we have noted, black females, white females, black males, and white males—as well as race-sex subgroups from other cultures—have their own unique problems and relevant issues. These factors must also be considered in any research into or treatment of racism or sexism.

Sedlacek, Brooks, Christensen, Harway, and Merritt

(1976), in a series of studies aimed at comparing racism and sexism, concluded that: (1) Men generally view women more positively than whites view blacks. (2) Sexism appears to be more a reluctance to view men and women outside their traditional roles than it is a negative feeling. (3) Situations involving women in occupational roles and dating behavior seem to generate the most general attitudes of men toward women. (4) Sexism, sexual attitudes, and sexual behavior seem to be relatively independent phenomena. (5) Perceptions of sex roles seem to be critical in understanding the relationships between black and white cultures.

We feel, therefore, that the most practical way to define sexism is as a specific case of racism, since our object is to understand a process we can apply to any group which is discriminated against—past, present, or future.

THE END OF RACISM

Obviously, our book is geared to this outcome. Whether it will ever come to pass on a large or total scale in the United States, or anywhere else, is gross conjecture at best. While there is much historical evidence that men and women have changed very little (we still have wars, poverty, inhumane treatment), there is a more positive view that says we are getting better with each decade and generation. Certainly a book such as this one would have been unthinkable a hundred or even fifty years ago. However, every racism fighter must guard against the tendency to view social causes as fads. Indeed, there are many in the United States who feel that we have got rid of racism against blacks and have gone too far, so that we now have "reverse discrimination." Watts and Free (1973) report that only mass transportation ranks lower than helping blacks as a domestic issue of concern to most Americans. Fifty-four percent of all Americans felt that programs to improve the situation of blacks should be kept at the present levels or reduced—and the Nixon administration's budgets reflected this recommendation. This was before the energy crisis and Watergate, but it should serve as a reminder that while the "popularity" of issues may shift, the realities of racism are still with us.

As a society, we have made progress at the outermost levels of the problem, but we still have many deeper layers of racism to resolve. Thus the challenge of this book, and our challenge to the reader, is to attack these deeper layers.

Answers to the
Dove Counterbalance General Intelligence Test

1. (d)	7. (c)	13. (c)	19. (c)	25. (c)
2. (e)	8. (c)	14. (c)	20. (c)	26. (c)
3. (c)	9. (d)	15. (d)	21. (d)	27. (c)
4. (c)	10. (c)	16. (d)	22. (c)	28. (a)
5. (a)	11. (d)	17. (b)	23. (a)	29. (e)
6. (d)	12. (c)	18. (c)	24. (b)	30. (b)

Appendix

We thank the following individuals for their participation in this role-playing session:

Sharon Bravy	Alice Handley
Christine Carrington	Javier Miyares
Paula Carroll	Janice Stevenson
Judy Clarke	Warwick Troy
David Fago	Rebecca Williams
Lois Wright	

See page 84 for a description of the roles and nature of the session.

Role D: We've gathered this committee in order to organize the school's curriculum, and I hope you'll introduce yourselves and let us know what you think are the important things to bring out about the curriculum. I'll chair the committee for this day.

Role C: I am a businessman in the community and I see my-
self as representing, I guess, that segment of the
community. I'm most concerned, really, about the
cost of education and I guess I'm approaching this
whole thing from a pretty pragmatic kind of perspective. I'm interested in getting the best education we can provide for our children with the least
cost and tax for local citizens. That's where I stand.

Role D: Are there some kinds of curricula that would be
more important to you than another as a business
person in the community? Perhaps you don't want
to respond to that now, but if you hear what the
others are about to present . . .

Role A: I'm a high school teacher and I'm very much concerned about the curriculum as it relates to black
people. I want to have a black studies—a very
strong black studies—program in the curriculum.

Role E: I don't know if you all know, but I'm a senior here
and I'm president of my class and I'm really concerned about this whole thing. Well, one of the reasons why I wanted to participate in the committee
was because I think the present curriculum is really
serving us quite well. I think we have a good high
school. I think if you'll look at the accomplishments
of the people who have gone on from here in the
past, there are a lot of people who have gone on to
college and are doing well, and I really feel that the
curriculum as it is is serving me and I think I speak
for the rest of my class. It's serving us very well and
I really wonder if we should mess with a good thing.

Role B: I definitely agree with what E said. I'm a parent—
not E's parent—but a parent serving on this committee and I strongly support tradition in the school
system, maintaining what we have. It's quite ap-

propriate; it worked well for me. I'm a very well educated person and I think it can work just as well for my children. I see no need for change and I think we can just go on from there.

Role D: I'm sure they understand your remarks but I want to go back to Mr. C's comments. Do you think that economically it's serving the community?

Role C: Yes, I think what we have is quite adequate, certainly. My initial feeling is to institute changes in the curriculum is only going to come with some added expense. Presumably, if we start making changes they're going to be experimental in nature and we don't know how they are going to work, and to me that means more money. I'm also concerned about the kind of changes you're going to make, and I'm really not clear about what people want in terms of changes in the curriculum. I feel that what we've had in the past has worked well for us. I don't know that there is any need to change.

Role A: Well, certainly black students would argue that point and I can speak for them. I think that there are no models, for example, throughout the whole educational history of most black children—black models, that is. And I feel that now these students are really pretty tired of having to read about black people solely in terms of deficit models. They want to see some of the things that blacks are doing, other than sweeping floors and washing dishes, and I feel that we are really disservicing—for lack of a better word—black students. And I think that a black studies course or a black studies program in the curriculum would help to change some of those historical problems.

Role B: I disagree completely with you, with what you've

said. I agree with what Mr. C said, that, separate from the money issue about changes in the curriculum, tradition is a strong force in the American culture and it's very important that we maintain tradition and that we pass on to our children the mores and values of our culture. I think that the black child in the classroom *does* have models in the society. Look at George Washington Carver and that man in Boston that was shot, Crispus Attucks. Now those are good models for the black child, and quite sufficient I think—no more than necessary. I think no changes are necessary at all.

Role A: What is the traditional American culture, as you see it?

Role B: Well, it's the one that I was raised by—patriotism, honor the flag, love my mom, good old apple pie. You know how that goes.

Role A: No, I don't know how it goes. (Laughter.)

Role E: As I said, I'm looking at this from a student's point of view, and what I want to get out of this high school is a good education so I can do well in college. That's really what I'm concerned about, and I think I understand about the difference in cultures, black culture and white culture and Asian-American culture and stuff, and I don't see anything wrong with knowing and understanding that. However, I really don't think that it's going to do me any good when I get to college to have a black studies course.

Role A: What do you think the black studies course would entail? What kinds of things do you think you would be studying?

Role E: Probably learning about black Americans, their contributions to our country.

Role A: Yes, OK. Well, their contributions to what, for example?

Role E: Well, to education, to music, art, anything. Whatever they contributed to.

Role A: Do you think this would not be helpful to you in understanding blacks? Do you feel you understand, for example, black people or a friend? Let's say a black *friend*—I don't want to say black *people*.

Role E: Sure. I mean I was elected president of my class, and don't you think that indicates that people realize that I understand? I have a black friend. Some of my best friends are black.

Role D: Miss A, I think that people really do understand what you are saying and they have been listening to you. But there seems to be a strong feeling that we should be economical and that the curriculum is satisfying the needs, and I tend to agree that there are good models set, whether they are black or white. I don't see why black students can't follow the models that are set by white heroes and by the stories that they read about white people. That seems to have served very well in the past.

Role A: Well, that's questionable. How has it served well in the past?

Role D: At this point, I think it might be valuable to go on to some other curriculum discussion.

Role A: Well, I don't think we've really moved anywhere on this discussion, so I really wouldn't like to move on to another discussion. I have a list here of about 100 black students who are really strongly opposed to what they are learning, and, speaking to E's remarks, I'm not sure that what you are learning is preparing you in the sense of being a full human being. I think that the statement you made about

a black studies course would probably give you—
tell you—some of the contributions that black
Americans made. I don't think that that's really the
purpose of the program, as I see it. I feel that the
students feel a lack of knowledge, not only about
the contributions of blacks but really about themselves as black, and I think that this curriculum
would help to enhance black students. It's not so
much that "All right, today we're going to learn
about black Americans and tomorrow we're going
to learn about white Americans," but it's just the
whole identification process that is lacking for black
students, simply because there are no models in the
textbooks or in the courses. And I really feel this
is a very crucial thing. I don't see how it's going to
really make that much difference economically.

Role C: Even aside from the economics, I really don't understand what you are really talking about when
you're talking about identification and models and
100 dissatisfied black students who want this course.

Role A: As representative of many others.

Role C: Well, I'm really concerned about this. I guess I'm
really concerned about the motives behind it. You're
talking about these abstract concepts that I don't
understand. It seems more to me like—well, I'm
really questioning the motives behind it. I don't
know if it's for education or organizing black students as a group in the school. I just see it causing
trouble. I see it as some sort of political—I don't
know. I just don't like the sound of it.

Role B: Even separate from that, black students in the past
have had models and these models have functioned
quite well, and there are many blacks who have
gone through the traditional education system and

succeeded quite well. For example, Mahalia Jackson. Now she was raised in American culture, as it was in the past, and succeeded quite well. Edward Brooke, a prominent senator in our country, who was raised in the American education system without these frills that you say are necessary—these students say are necessary—did quite well. Barry Gordy has his own business in Detroit—one of our outstanding businessmen. Then that guy in the Olympics in Hitler's day who was a black who did quite well—had a little trouble, but we'll ignore that. Jim Brown did quite well in athletics. There are many black models available for black students today to use. I think these are quite sufficient without instigating any changes in our curriculum. As a parent, I would not see any need to change the way my child is educated.

Role A: Would you agree that we are living in a white racist culture, that white racism is alive and well?

Role B: I think that in the past this country could be accused of some racist policies. However, I think great progress has been made.

Role A: No, I mean *now;* do you feel *now* that white racism is alive and functioning?

Role B: I don't think you can do it like that. I think you have to look at it on a continuum.

Role C: Is that what you're saying this course is for then, to combat racism?

Role A: Combat it? I don't know what combating it would mean but I certainly think it could point up many of the contradictions that we all are a part of. I think the course, number 1, would help to give black students, as I said, a sense of being a part of the educational process, as opposed to something outside looking in. I think this is what many black students have said to me. They feel that the textbooks and the theories—you know, the whole approach—is something that they don't feel a part of. They don't feel that they've contributed anything because there are no models for this; so they are learning about something they don't feel a part of, which as we all know, I'm sure, is not a good way to learn or doesn't help to enhance the individual.

Role C: What's that got to do with racism?

Role A: What has what got to do with racism?

Role C: Students feeling that they are outside.

Role A: Well, the fact that the textbooks have not included the significant contributions of blacks must say something about the phenomenon of racism. Would you agree with that? The fact that they have been systematically left out of the textbooks, for example, says to me that there is something operating here that we might want to look at.

Role E: I'm having real problems here because I'm looking at high school as something that's supposed to prepare me for competing in the job market or doing well in college, and I still don't understand what a black studies course is going to do to help me get better grades in college, which is what I'm really after. And I'm sure—speaking for the rest of my class, of which I am president—I really feel like I'm speaking for the black members of my class too, who want to be as well prepared as they possibly can to compete in the world.

Role A: Well, first of all I don't think you can speak for the black members of your class, or even your class. I think you have to speak for yourself. I keep hearing you say that high school is going to prepare you for college and prepare you for competing. How does a black studies curriculum interfere with that process? Do you see this as an either/or? In other words, the courses that will prepare you will be what, for example?

Role E: Algebra.

Role A: OK.

Role E: Biology.

Role B: I agree with what E has said completely. It's only necessary for her to succeed in college that she have the traditional systems—reading, writing, and arithmetic. Those do not reflect race in any way; so as long as she is getting these in her education system, she's getting all that's necessary. And that goes for the black students, too, in order to succeed in college.

Role A: No, it doesn't go for the black students.

Role B: If they can read, if they can do arithmetic, if they can write—this is what's necessary. This has always worked in our system, and it will always continue to work.

Role A: Is your opinion an ordinary or expert one?

Role B: I beg your pardon?

Role A: Is your opinion ordinary or expert?

Role B: My opinion is of one who has succeeded in this system.

Role D: I think that we really have a lot of understanding for some of the things you've said. Though some of the things, I agree, are a little vague, like education for the whole person. I rather think E's right, that we are looking for a way to get people to college and to help them find jobs, and I haven't heard you say anything in any specific way that would be helpful to a black student or a white student in your black studies program. Can you be a little more specific about the things that would point toward the goals that the other members of the committee seem to think are quite important?

Role C: OK, tell me how much it's going to cost.

Role A: Well, I think maybe first we should talk about the goals of education, of high school education, as you see them. Is that the only goal, or should that be the only goal, to prepare students to get into college? Do you see education in high school as something to get through quickly to get to college? Is that what you see as the goal of education?

Role D: No, I certainly see it as a very important experience for the students. They learn lots of social things, they learn responsibilities, such as being class president. There are many important things for them to learn, but it hasn't been illustrated to me that black studies should be any part of this. Most of the things they need to know how to do—to socialize, to assume responsibility as good citizens, as well as the basic things that have been brought up: reading, writing, and arithmetic—are accomplished in the high school.

Role A: Well, maybe we should break it down. You know, we keep saying black studies. Maybe we should talk about a course that I would see as important. One course could be something like understanding other cultures. It would not necessarily be whites understanding black culture but also an understanding between the people in classes about individual differences which may be cultural.

Role D: We have geography since the fifth grade.

Role A: I hardly think geography would suffice. I can't remember any blacks mentioning that particular text-book. I think I can see one course as being very important.

Role B: What about that guy John Henry?

Role A: What about him?

Role B: He's mentioned in the geography book. He did great things.

Role A: Well, I don't remember it, so it must not have men-tioned him very much. The point is, I think a course that would speak to just the interrelationships be-tween blacks and whites in the school would be a very important course. Black studies itself really doesn't, you know. We can't get to all the courses in the curriculum, but I certainly think a course dealing with the interpersonal relationships between blacks and whites would be a very significant course to have in the curriculum.

Role D: Don't you think a course like this would become very personal and take us away from the broad, general things we are trying to teach students?

Role A: Well, I don't quite understand that as a goal. I think part of education is interpersonal. I think part of becoming educated is learning how to get along with other people.

Role B: I think that the social things about which both of you ladies are speaking are not the business of the school at all. They are not the business of the class-room. Traditionally, these forces can be handled outside the school room. For example, community forces, like the church, have always dealt with social issues—like the youth clubs, the scout troops. Now these are the vehicles that can serve as the outlet for black students relating to white students. I think this is quite appropriate, and I don't think it's necessary to bring these things into the classroom.

Role C: I agree. It sounds like trouble to me, and it sounds like it's going to cost a lot of money. And I do not see any concrete benefits.

Role A: What kind of trouble does it sound like?

Role C: It sounds to me like you're going to start stirring up a lot of trouble, and it's going to cause problems among the students. Because I can see just black students in one course and white students in another course, and I can see a lot of friction being produced by that. I don't know a whole lot about education, what goes on in the school, but my reaction is to say I don't like the way it sounds, and it sounds like it is going to cost a lot of money. Hearing that students have done very well, given the existing kind of programs we have, what good is it?

Role B: Absolutely.

Role A: Done very well how? I'm just confused. You say that . . .

Role D: We are going to have to bring this committee meeting to a close. We haven't addressed ourselves to some of the important things, like how we are going to equip the soccer team or what we are going to be teaching in English next year. We appreciate your bringing your views here. I hope you have understood that we are not ready to experiment to get into anything costly, and we don't want to breach the parents' prerogative of teaching these social things at home. We think that's appropriate. We'll talk about the other matters at the next meeting.

Role C: Yes, particularly if the soccer team—the soccer team doesn't have any equipment? That's shocking!

Role B: They've had such a good year.

DISCUSSION LEADER:

OK; now I'd like to ask the people who were observing that, what do you think was going on there? Who has some comment on what they thought was happening?

OBSERVER 1:

People weren't saying what they really felt, you know, like C talking about economics when that really wasn't his concern. And I think he demonstrated that at the end.

LEADER:

He was talking about economics but that really was not his . . .

OBSERVER 1:

I think that was just an example of his "own thing." I think he was just using that as an excuse.

OBSERVER 2:

Are you saying that he didn't believe in the role he was playing, or in fact he unrealistically portrayed the role—that no one could feel the things he claimed to feel?

OBSERVER 1:

I think he played the role well and I think it's a real role, OK? What I'm saying is that if it had been a real concern when someone said "Well, the soccer team needs equipment, and that means money" the response wouldn't have been "Well, we got to get the equipment." It would be "Equipment is of concern but see how much it costs." It would have been a congruent response.

LEADER:

Any other comments? What I heard you saying was that you seem to be questioning the motives of the person. You want to think in terms of the earlier stages of the model that we talked about. Do we really want to deal with motives or do we want to deal with the outcome? Think about C's position. In essence, what we were saying earlier was that it doesn't really make any difference why he was taking that position, that the outcome would be negative and racist by our earlier definitions. Anybody see anything else happening here they might want to comment on before we get to specific roles?

OBSERVER 3:

I felt that A, when various other members were displaying their roles, kept picking up what it was that she wanted to get across, instead of the student, for instance, who kept saying that I'm getting what I want out of it. I might have approached it a little differently by saying I can show you a way that you can get more than this, as opposed to challenging her position. Accept her position as being a legitimate one and then give her an additional thing of expanding this.

OBSERVER 4:

I really think that C was a bit surprised at his role, but I learned something from this: that if you want to say something like this you should have an estimated cost for somebody like the businessman, advantages for the student, the things that the mother might be worried about. A very clear-cut thing instead of maybe going to the emotional.

LEADER:

That is a good point. Let's pick up on that. If you were going to come back at the next meeting and maybe deal with these same issues, which might have been inferred, can we each come up with a couple of things about each of these roles that might be key things or ways to reach these other people? If we were trying to argue for the black studies curriculum and support the role of A, what might we come up with for each of these role players?

OBSERVER 2:

Certainly, I think, A should have checked out the sort of potential opposition her role was going to draw from her audience and addressed herself specifically to the right of the traditional arguments of B and E—that is, of the parent and the student—and come up with some detail, some homework, some facts and figures. For instance, what was impressive, I thought, about the role playing is that for once you got a situation where A argued her case extremely convincingly. One is tempted to believe that is in fact her position. Of course, it may have been her extremely good role playing. What you usually don't get is that people in opposition also argue some extremely convincing arguments for a traditional case. So it was in fact a viable debate, and one could imagine that A, in preparing for this, would know the mettle of her adversaries and would have planned ahead and dropped a few bones, a few rewards. For instance, I've checked with a lot of whites and they are interested in getting to know some of the blacks too. So give them something they can use, because it's going to be a mixture of sensations from all the others.

LEADER:

Let's think about each role one at a time. Of course, we had the advocate in role A that you all picked up and commented on. What about role C, which was the businessman? How did you perceive that person? Was there anything that would be particularly important or unimportant about dealing with somebody like that in the future?

OBSERVER 2:

One of the important things would be the extent to which new programs could be initiated in the school by using the existing resources. In other words, it's simply a matter of reallocating resources. In other words, C could be mollified if you like, seduced into not being such a formidable enemy of the proposition—if A could have come up with specific plans for using existing resources to achieve her goal, rather than requiring the objectionable use of finances. That would have impressed C mainly as a responsible act. C is committed to responsibility in the status quo. C presumably would have less . . .

LEADER:

OK; we wouldn't be surprised to find somebody like C in an advisory group or community group or something like that. How about the student role, role E? How would you analyze that kind of person?

OBSERVER 2:

Well, I suppose one of the things that could be suggested in E's role is that the value system seemed to imply that the three *R*'s were the crucial thing. Not only the crucial thing in an education but they predicted college success, in her eyes, which was something she personally valued very much. In fact there are a number of studies that show that by no means are they the sole viable predictors and that getting along with one's fellow man in increasingly complex social institutions, such as universities, is extremely important. In fact, who was to know what her interest will do in terms of changing? So E is shutting off her educational options very, very low, and she is clearly an intelligent woman and a leader. So I would have thought that an argument that would appeal to such a student would be to say "Look, you've got a great deal to accomplish by not setting your sights so low. Granted your ideas are good, but couldn't they be expanded? And here's how it could be done."

LEADER:

Again, would that be a surprising role for somebody like a class president to take?

OBSERVER 5:

I thought she was very convincing.

LEADER:

She was convincing?

OBSERVER 5:

Yes. Given her goal to go to college and the status she had attained already, why should she need black studies?

LEADER:

Well, we are thinking about strategies in the future. It's often a common mistake to figure the students are really in favor of all kinds of change. Sometimes that's true, but quite often you'll find the formal student leadership has as much at stake in the institution, in the way it is right now, as anybody else—as a principal, etc.

OK. How about role B? Who has a comment on that—what was happening?

OBSERVER 4:

I was surprised by the amazing knowledge she had

of black personalities. I tend to think a typical parent wouldn't know so much of black history as she did.

OBSERVER 2:

On the other hand, she said she was a leader and extremely well educated. She was also on the committee, and I would have thought that the people who wanted to get this woman's attention would have done some homework about her qualities. She was very impressive indeed; really a top adversary. She had a rather traditional viewpoint, but the ammunition she defended herself with wasn't traditional. It was up to the mark and she had prepared herself well. It's people like her who are one of the biggest obstacles to any sort of change. She was making an argument convincingly for the status quo, in a compelling way, in a way that appeals to more people.

LEADER:

So B had some information and she used it very well, which makes it that much harder to act like an expert if you're in A's position, trying to convince other people, because there is good opposition.

What did you think about the role of D? What kind of a leader was this person, as you saw it? What observations do you have?

OBSERVER 6:

I think D let things get away from her. She started out by saying this was a meeting to discuss curriculum, if I remember correctly, and then the discussion went all over the field. Nobody pinned down that if you are going to decide on a curriculum for something, you first have to decide what you're trying to teach, what your educational goals are, and how

the present curriculum meets or does not meet them.
We never heard any of that. We just heard everybody's opinion on the subject. I thought the leader
could have pulled that in a little more. It might
have helped.

LEADER:

What did the leader do then?

OBSERVER 6:

Later on, when she summed up, she seemed to take
sides. It just seemed to me that a chairman would
have said "Well, now wait a minute; let's . . ."

OBSERVER 4:

It seems to me that if the majority in the committee
had wanted black studies, the principal would have
favored black studies. It seemed like she was just
taking the majority's view to keep her position, or
whatever, and not to be efficient.

OBSERVER 2:

It seemed to me that she was a chairperson that was
trying to push the meeting along, and she was under
time restraints and she recognized that it was a one-
sided debate, not in terms of the quality of the debate but in terms of the for or against.

OBSERVER 7:

I was wondering why, when you set up the role-
playing situation, you set it up in such a way that
there was not at least one supporter of the . . .

LEADER:

Based on what we have covered so far in the model,
why would you think that we would set up the role
that way?

OBSERVER 6:

That sort of typifies society right now, I think. If
you get one person with her role, with her viewpoint

on the school board—well, in this area anyway—
you are going to be surprised at one person taking
that position.

LEADER:

OK; that's a good point. We're kind of trying to set
you up for the next two stages, which are going to
deal with goals and strategies, and what we're suggesting by this role-playing situation is that it's going
to be tough sledding, no matter what you do, and
the types of opposition you face are not going to be
monolithic or uniform. You are going to get opposition from all different quarters. The results of
that opposition might all be the same, but you may
have to counter each type of opposition in a different way. So this is a kind of miniexample of how
you may have to fight a lot of different forces if you
are trying to change anything that some of us may
consider fairly noninnovative or nonradical, like a
black studies program. Particularly in these days,
when there seems to be a swing back toward traditional education, the three *R*'s and so forth. I think
it's probably going to be tougher to set up a program like this than it was four or five years ago. So
if you're serious about it, you've got to line up your
ducks and be willing to face some of that opposition.

Before we get any further, I'd like to have each
person read their role. Just for our discussion purposes, let's have each person read their role and state
any reactions they had. The participants can respond also.

[Role A is read.]

LEADER:

OK. That's pretty much what everybody thought
you were going to do.

[Role C is read.]

OBSERVER 5:

It came across very well. I wrote a comment on C's presentation: "Don't rock the boat."

LEADER:

I think all of you got that. Obviously, he spoke more eloquently than each of you might have about educational problems; but I think you caught yourself once there, C, and said "Man, I don't know what you mean by roles and self-concept and all that kind of jargon." And, certainly, someone in your position probably would never have heard the terms, let alone understood what they mean.

[Role E is read.]

LEADER:

That's pretty much what we thought.

[Role B is read.]

PARTICIPANT B:

I want to respond to something Observer 4 said— evidence that I tried to defend my position strongly. I tried to limit the evidence I picked up to white schools; so the things I used were as available to a white parent as to a black parent.

OBSERVER 6:

B, I knew everything you said, and I'm not an expert on blacks.

LEADER:

Yes, but you know more than you'd find typically.

OBSERVER 5:

What she mentioned were things I knew, that I picked up along the way.

OBSERVER 7:

I think leading off with Mahalia Jackson was really in character.

PARTICIPANT A:

My reaction was that I didn't want to deal with that.

I didn't want to deal with "counter" names and with what blacks feel because that wasn't going to get us anywhere. I wanted to focus more on educational goals, rather than on how many blacks you can name and how many did this or that. And I guess I was kind of looking for the chairperson to get into that, but then, realizing she didn't want it either, I purposely did not react because that's typical. You know, let's point out four or five blacks who have made it and then, you know, why can't all the others? So I had a very highly emotional charge and my reaction was not to react.

OBSERVER 6:

I felt that somewhere around the table I got a list of about seven goals that were tossed in. One of them was getting along with one another socially. That was pretty much downgraded. It seems to me that someone should have picked up on that. Anyway, from my point of view, one of the most important reasons that a community pays for education is to educate these people to be good citizens, and in order to be a good citizen you have to get along with the people with whom you live and in your community. That's very important.

PARTICIPANT A:

I tried to pick up on that. One of the things that concerned me was black studies. You know that has a sort of kind of thing, what is black studies. Say let's look at one course, let's look at a course in interpersonal relationships. It could be understanding other cultures, not a course where I'm going to learn about fifty black people and what they did that wasn't mentioned in a white textbook. So my concern was really to narrow it to a course that could be beneficial to blacks, whites, whatever— rather than this thing called black studies, which I think none of us really quite understands. I don't.

LEADER:

That's a good point of strategy, which we'll also get to. Get specific wherever you can so that you can get people to agree on a point rather than a general idea. Probably you would have a tough time trying to get a businessman to accept the idea that you ought to be studying black something-or-other, but if you could convince him that the course was cheap and everybody didn't have to take it, he might go along with it.

OBSERVER 6:

For example, if he didn't have black kids throwing rocks through his windows—because they had learned to get along with one another. That would be an angle that a businessman could consider.

PARTICIPANT A:

Why would we have to convince the businessman anyway?

LEADER:

Well, this committee had the power to essentially recommend or reject the curriculum. Many schools have some kind of committee like this, which, if it doesn't have formal power, has informal power, so that if they give a negative recommendation, nothing is going to get through—especially if you have a principal or leader like you've got in this particular group. That is, who's concerned about reflecting what the community, students, and parents want.

OBSERVER 6:

We didn't hear D's role. I would like to hear what she was supposed to do.

[Role D is read.]

PARTICIPANT D:

I would like to comment that I added my own observation of high school principals and other administrators, who announce frequently—at this meeting by their presence or by their words—that they are in power. And they close it with some statement of power, but throughout the meeting they assume no responsibility for the decisions at all. So they are "humble public servants" who are only doing as the public asks.

PARTICIPANT A:

You portrayed that beautifully.

PARTICIPANT B:

It was very difficult.

LEADER:

Is there anyone else who would like to make any last comments?

OBSERVER 5:

I was wondering why A did not address herself to the comment that social interaction and interpersonal relationships, etc., etc., do not belong in the school—that they belong in the home and the church and whatnot.

PARTICIPANT A:

I couldn't get in, for one thing. Somebody else picked it up. I tried to go back there because I really wanted to deal with the emotionality rather than get into facts and figures. That's going to make a difference because I think it's a heavily emotionally charged thing, but I couldn't get into that because "Mother" was rambling.

LEADER:

The last point. One of the things we'll also deal with is to try to reduce emotionality, rather than counter an emotional argument with another emotional argument, which will probably take you off where you'll never get anything done. Try to do just the kinds of things that you've been suggesting. Try to come up with information. Tone down the whole thing so you can stick to something specific, rather than have just a shouting match. Once you get to that aspect of the ball game, it's probably over as far as you're concerned.

OBSERVER 2:

The high school teacher, who wanted a black studies program, should have avoided using words like "educational values" and "goals" when, in fact, the others didn't want to hear things like that. What she should have done, had she been better prepared, would be to find out just what sort of reinforcements operated for those people. If she was dealing with a group of her peers, even some with different value systems, her arguments would have been great; but it didn't work at all.

LEADER:

OK; very good. Thank you all.

Bibliography

Adams, M. "The Compassion Trap." In V. Gornick and B. K. Moran (eds.), *Women in Sexist Society: Studies in Power and Powerlessness*. New York: Basic Books, 1971.

Adorno, T. W., Frenkel-Brunswik, E., Levinson, D. J., and Sanford, R. N. *The Authoritarian Personality*. New York: Harper & Row, 1950.

Alinsky, S. D. *Rules for Radicals*. New York: Random House, 1971.

Allport, G. W. *The Nature of Prejudice*. Garden City, N.Y.: Anchor-Doubleday, 1958.

Amir, Y. "Contact Hypothesis in Ethnic Relations," *Psychological Bulletin* (1969), 71: 319–342.

Baird, L. L. "A Portrait of Blacks in Graduate Studies." *Findings* (1974), 2: 1–4.

Ball, H. W. "Racial Attitudes of White Educators in a Situational Context." Unpublished M.A. thesis, University of Maryland, 1971.

Banks, J. A. "The Need for Positive Racial Attitudes in Textbooks." In R. L. Green, *Racial Crisis in American Education*. Chicago: Follett, 1969.

Baratz, J. C. "Language Abilities of Black Americans." In K. S. Miller and R. M. Dreger (eds.), *Comparative Studies of Blacks and Whites in the United States*. New York: Seminar Press, 1973.

Barney, P. O., and Hall, L. D. "A Study in Discrimination." *Personnel and Guidance Journal* (1965), 44: 707–709.

Berger, S. E., and Tedeschi, J. T. "Race of Delinquent and Dependent Children and Opportunity Costs as Factors in Aggressive Play in the Prisoner's Dilemma Game." Paper presented to the Southeastern Psychological Association, Roanoke, Va., April 1968.

Birk, J. M., Barbanel, L., Brooks, L., Herman, M. H., Juhasz, J. B., Seltzer, R. A., and Tangri, S. S. "A Content Analysis of Sexual Bias in Commonly Used Psychological Textbooks." (Mimeograph) University of Maryland, 1974.

Brooks, G. C., Jr. "The Effect of Occupation on the Measurement of Racial Attitudes." Unpublished Ph.D. dissertation, University of Maryland, 1971.

————. "A Pilot Study of Racial Attitudes and Behavioral Changes of University Residence Hall Staff." Paper presented at the American Personnel and Guidance Association Convention, Chicago, March 27, 1972.

————, and Sedlacek, W. E. "An Experimental Study of Differential Reactions of Whites Toward Negroes and Blacks." *American Psychological Association Proceedings* (1970), 5: 359–360.

————. "Choice of Racial Referent as a Variable in Racial Attitude Measurement." *Cultural Study Center Research Report No. 5–71,* University of Maryland, 1971.

————. "The Role of Occupational Information in Racial Attitude Measurement." *Cultural Study Center Research Report No. 5–72,* University of Maryland, 1972.

————, and Chaples, E. A. "A Cross-cultural Comparison of Danish and U.S. Racial Attitudes." *Cultural Study Center*

Research Report No. 10–71, University of Maryland, 1971. Also in *American Psychological Association Proceedings* (1972), 7: 283–284.

————. "A Cross-cultural Comparison of Danish and U.S. Attitudes toward Minority Groups." *Research in Higher Education* (1974), 2: 207–220.

Brooks, G. C., Jr., Sedlacek, W. E., and Mindus, L. A. "Interracial Contact and Attitudes Among University Students." *Journal of Non-White Concerns in Personnel and Guidance* (1973), 1: 102–110.

Burrell, L., and Rayder, N. F. "Black and White Students' Attitudes Toward White Counselors." *Journal of Negro Education* (1971), 20: 48–52.

Chaples, E. A., Sedlacek, W. E., and Brooks, G. C., Jr. "Measuring Prejudicial Attitudes in a Situational Context: A Report on a Danish Experiment." *Scandinavian Political Studies* (1972), 7: 235–247.

————. "Prejudicial Attitudes of Danish Students: Some Educational Implications." Paper presented at the American Educational Research Association Convention, New Orleans, Feb. 28, 1973.

Chapman, T. H. "Simulation Game Effects on Attitudes Regarding Racism and Sexism." Unpublished Ph.D. dissertation, University of Maryland, 1974.

Chesler, M. A. "Teacher Training Designs for Improving Instruction in Interracial Classrooms." *Journal of Applied Behavioral Science* (1971) 7: 612–641.

Christensen, K. C., and Sedlacek, W. E. "Differential Faculty Attitudes Toward Blacks, Females and Students in General." *Journal of the National Association of Women Deans, Administrators and Counselors* (1974), 37: 78–84.

Clark, K. B. *Prejudice and Your Child.* Boston: Beacon Press, 1963.

————, and Plotkin, L. *The Negro Student at Integrated Colleges.* New York: National Scholarship Service and Fund for Negro Students, 1964.

Cleary, T. A. "Test Bias: Prediction of Grades of Negro and

White Students in Integrated Colleges." *Journal of Educational Measurement* (1968), 5: 115–124.

Cleaver, E. *Soul on Ice.* New York: Dell, 1968.

Cole, N. S. "Bias in Selection." *Journal of Educational Measurement* (1973), 10: 237–255.

Coleman, J. S., Campbell, E. Q., Hobson, C. J., McPartland, J., Mood, A. M., Weinfield, F. D., and York, R. L. *Equality of Educational Opportunity.* Washington, D.C.: U.S. Government Printing Office, 1966.

Collins, A. M., and Sedlacek, W. E. "Counselor Ratings of Male and Female Clients." *Journal of the National Association of Women Deans, Administrators and Counselors* (1974), 37: 128–132.

Comer, J. P. *Beyond Black and White.* New York: Quadrangle, 1972.

Culbertson, F. M. "Modification of an Emotionally Held Attitude Through Role Playing." *Journal of Abnormal and Social Psychology* (1957), 54: 230–233.

Daniels, R., and Kitano, H. H. L. *American Racism: Exploration of the Nature of Prejudice.* Englewood Cliffs, N.J.: Prentice-Hall, 1970.

D'Costa, A., Bashook, P., Elliott, P., Jarecky, R., Leavell, W., Prieto, D., and Sedlacek, W. E. *Simulated Minority Admissions Exercises Workbook.* Washington, D.C.: Association of American Medical Colleges, 1974.

————. *Simulated Minority Admissions Exercise Workbook: Analysis and Discussion.* Washington, D.C.: Association of American Medical Colleges, 1975.

DeFleur, M. L., and Wester, F. R. "Verbal Attitudes and Overt Acts: An Experiment on the Scheme of Attitudes." *American Sociological Action* (1958), 23: 667–673.

DiCesare, A., Sedlacek, W. E., and Brooks, G. C., Jr. "Nonintellectual Correlates of Black Student Attrition." *Journal of College Student Personnel* (1972), 13: 319–324.

Downs, A. *Racism in America and How to Combat It.* Washington, D.C.: U.S. Commission on Civil Rights, U.S. Government Printing Office, 1970.

Eberly, C. G. "Racial Attitudes of Michigan State University Freshmen." Paper presented at the American Personnel and Guidance Association Convention, Chicago, March 27, 1972a.

————. "An Alternative Analysis for the Situational Attitude Scale." *Office of Evaluation Services Research Report No. 5,* Michigan State University, 1972b.

Ehrlich, H. J. *The Social Psychology of Prejudice.* New York: Wiley, 1973.

Ellison, R. *The Invisible Man.* New York: New American Library, 1953.

Epps, E. G. "Correlates of Academic Achievement among Northern and Southern Urban Negro Students." *Journal of Social Issues* (1969), 25: 5–13.

Farver, A. S., Sedlacek, W. E., and Brooks, G. C., Jr. "Longitudinal Predictions of Black and White University Student Grades." *Measurement and Evaluation in Guidance* (1975), 7: 243–250.

Fendrich, J. M. "A Study of Whites' Attitudes, Commitment, and Overt Behavior Toward Members of a Minority Group." Unpublished Ph.D. dissertation, Michigan State University, 1965.

————. "A Study of the Association Among Attitudes, Commitment and Overt Behavior in Different Experimental Situations." *Social Forces* (1967), 45: 347–355.

Franklin, J. H. *From Slavery to Freedom.* New York: Knopf, 1967.

Gardner, J. L. "Sexist Counseling Must Stop." *Personnel and Guidance Journal* (1971), 49: 705–714.

Gardner, J. W. *Self-renewal: The Individual and the Innovative Society.* New York: Harper & Row, 1965.

————. "Common Cause." *Report from Washington* (1971), 1(10).

Glock, C. Y., and Siegelman, E. *Prejudice, U.S.A.* New York: Praeger, 1969.

———— and Stark, R. *Christian Beliefs and Anti-Semitism.* New York: Harper & Row, 1966.

Golden, H. *Only in America.* New York: World, 1958.

Gossett, T. F. *Race: The History of an Idea in America.* Dallas, Tex.: Southern Methodist University Press, 1963.

Green, R. L. "After School Integration—What? Problems in Social Learning." *Personnel and Guidance Journal* (1966), 45: 704–710.

————, and Farquhar, W. W. "Negro Academic Motivation and Scholastic Achievement." *Journal of Educational Psychology* (1965), 56: 241–243.

Grier, W. H., and Cobbs, P. M. *Black Rage.* New York: Bantam, 1968.

Gurin, P., Gurin G., Lao, R., and Beattie, M. "Internal-External Control in the Motivational Dynamics of Negro Youth." *Journal of Social Issues* (1969), 3: 29–53.

Hanson, G. R., Belcher, L., Sedlacek, W. E., and Thrush, R. *Alternatives to a Moratorium on Testing: An ACPA Commission IX Position Paper on Test Bias in the College Setting.* Washington, D.C.: American College Personnel Association, 1973.

Hartnagel, T. F. "Father Absence and Self-conception Among Lower Class White and Negro Boys." *Social Problems* (1970), 18: 152–163.

Hedman, A. R. "The Effect of a Selected Racism Training Program on the Verbal Behavior of White Teachers." Unpublished Ph.D. dissertation, University of Maryland, 1975.

Herman, M. H., and Sedlacek, W. E. "Sexist Attitudes Among Male University Students." *Journal of College Student Personnel* (1973a), 14: 544–548.

————. "Student Perceptions of the Need for a Women's Studies Program." *College Student Journal* (1973b), 7(3): 3–6.

————. "Career Orientation of High School and University Women." *Journal of the National Association of Women Deans, Administrators and Counselors* (1974a), 37: 161–166.

————. "Female University Student and Staff Perceptions of Rape." *Journal of the National Association of Women*

Deans, Administrators and Counselors (1974b), 38: 20–23.

Hernton, C. C. *Sexism and Racism in America.* New York: Grove Press, 1965.

Hesburgh, T. M. "Foreword." In C. Y. Glock and E. Siegelman (eds.), *Prejudice, U.S.A.* New York: Praeger, 1969.

Horowitz, J. L., Sedlacek, W. E., and Brooks, G. C., Jr. "Correlates of Black and White University Grades Beyond the Freshman Year." *Cultural Study Center Research Report No. 7–72,* University of Maryland, 1972a.

―――. "Repeated Measures Effects in Racial Attitude Measurement." *Cultural Study Center Research Report No. 8–72,* University of Maryland, 1972b.

Hyman, H. H. "Inconsistencies as a Problem of Attitude Measurement." *Journal of Social Issues* (1949), 5: 38–42.

Jackson, J. J. "Family Organization and Technology." In K. S. Miller and R. M. Dreger (eds.), *Comparative Studies of Blacks and Whites in the United States.* New York: Seminar Press, 1973.

Jensen, A. R. "How Much Can We Boost IQ and Scholastic Achievement?" *Harvard Educational Review* (1969), 39: 1–123.

Johnson, K. R. "The Language of Black Children: Instructional Implications." In R. L. Green, *Racial Crisis in American Education.* Chicago: Follett, 1969.

King, B. T., and Janis, I. L. "Comparison of the Effectiveness of Improvised versus Non-improvised Role Playing in Producing Opinion Changes." *Human Relations* (1956), 9: 177–186.

Knowles, L. L., and Prewitt, K. *Institutional Racism in America.* Englewood Cliffs, N.J.: Prentice-Hall, 1969.

Lefcourt, H. M., and Ladwig, G. W. "The American Negro: A Problem in Expectancies." *Journal of Personality and Social Psychology* (1965), 1: 377–380.

Leitner, D. W., and Sedlacek, W. E. "Characteristics of Successful Campus Police Officers." *Counseling Center Research Report No. 10–74,* University of Maryland, 1974.

Lewis, J. A., and Sedlacek, W. E. "The Relationship of Racial and Religious Attitudes Among University Students." *Cultural Study Center Research Report No. 8–73,* University of Maryland, 1973.

Linn, R. L. "Fair Test Use in Selection." *Review of Educational Research* (1973), 43: 139–161.

Maslow, A. H. *Motivation and Personality.* New York: Harper, 1954.

Merritt, M. S., Sedlacek, W. E., and Brooks, G. C., Jr. "Quality of Interracial Interaction Among University Students." *Cultural Study Center Research Report No. 6–74,* University of Maryland, 1974.

Moynihan, D. P. *The Negro Family: A Case for National Action.* Washington, D.C.: U.S. Government Printing Office, 1965.

Nader, R. "Corporate Violence Against the Consumer." In W. Osborne, *The Hope of the Powerless.* New York: Gordon and Breach, 1971.

————. "In the Public Interest: Student Activists." *New Republic* (1972), 166(8): 10–11.

Noar, G. *Sensitizing Teachers to Ethnic Groups.* New York: Allyn & Bacon, 1972.

Nobers, D. R. "The Effects of Father Absence and Mothers' Characteristics on the Identification of Adolescent White and Negro Males." Unpublished Ph.D. dissertation, St. Louis University, 1968.

Pfeifer, C. M., Jr., and Sedlacek, W. E. "Non-intellectual Correlates of Black and White Student Grades at the University of Maryland." *Cultural Study Center Research Report No. 3–70,* University of Maryland, 1970.

————. "The Validity of Academic Predictors for Black and White Students at a Predominantly White University." *Journal of Educational Measurement* (1971), 8: 253–261.

————. "Predicting Black Student Grades with Non-intellectual Measures." *Journal of Negro Education* (1974), 43: 67–76.

Report of the National Advisory Commission on Civil Disorders. New York: Grosset, 1968.

Roberts, S. O., and Horton, C. P. "Extent of and Effects of Desegregation." In K. S. Miller and R. M. Dreger (eds.), *Comparative Studies of Blacks and Whites in the United States.* New York: Seminar Press, 1973.

Rokeach, M. "The Nature and Meaning of Dogmatism." *Psychological Review* (1954), 61: 194–204.

Rosenthal, R., and Jacobson, L. "Self-fulfilling Prophecies in the Classroom: Teachers' Expectations as Unintended Determinants of Pupils' Intellectual Competence." In M. Deutsch, I. Katz, and A. R. Jensen (eds.), *Social Class, Race, and Psychological Development.* New York: Holt, Rinehart & Winston, 1968.

Rothenberg, P. J. "Locus of Control, Social Class, and Risk-taking in Negro Boys." *Dissertation Abstracts* (1968), 29(1-B): 379.

Rovner, R., and Sedlacek, W. E. "A Study of a Simplified Version of the Situational Attitude Scale (SAS)." *Cultural Study Center Research Report No. 7–74,* University of Maryland, 1974.

Rubovits, P. C., and Maehr, M. L. "Pygmalion Black and White." *Journal of Personality and Social Psychology* (1973), 25: 210–218.

Schwartz, B. N., and Disch, R. *White Racism: Its History, Pathology and Practice.* New York: Dell, 1970.

Sedlacek, W. E. "Uses of the Situational Attitude Scale (SAS) in Assessing Social Change." Paper presented at the American Personnel and Guidance Association Convention, Chicago, March 27, 1972.

———. *Racism in Society: A Behavioral Model for Change.* Teaneck, N.J.: Behavioral Sciences Tape Library, 1974 (No. 82220).

———. "Issues in Predicting Black Student Success in Higher Education." *Journal of Negro Education* (1975), 43: 512–516.

———, and Brooks, G. C., Jr. "Black Freshmen in Large Colleges: A Survey." *Personnel and Guidance Journal* (1970a), 49: 307–312.

_____. "Measuring Racial Attitudes in a Situational Context." *Psychological Reports* (1970b), 27: 971–980.

_____. "The Importance of Social Acceptability in the Measurement of Racial Attitudes." *Cultural Study Center Research Report No. 8–70,* University of Maryland, 1970c.

_____. "The Development of a Measure of Racial Attitudes." *Experimental Publication System, American Psychological Association,* MS 177C (1970d), vol. 5. Also in *Counseling Center Research Report No. 10–69,* University of Maryland, 1969. Also abstract in *American Psychological Association Proceedings* (1970d), 5: 161–162.

_____. "The Measurement of Attitudes of Whites Toward Blacks with Certain Beliefs." *Cultural Study Center Research Report No. 7–70,* University of Maryland, 1970e.

_____. "Social Acceptability in the Measurement of Racial Attitudes." *Psychological Reports* (1971a), 29: 17–18.

_____. "Race as an Experimenter Effect in Racial Attitude Measurement." *Cultural Study Center Research Report No. 1–71,* University of Maryland, 1971b.

_____. "Differences in Racial Attitudes of White Males and Females." *Cultural Study Center Research Report No. 2–72.* University of Maryland, 1972a.

_____. *Situational Attitude Scale (SAS) Manual.* Chicago: Natresources, 1972b.

_____. "Racial Attitudes, Authoritarianism and Dogmatism Among University Students." *College Student Journal* (1972c), 6(1): 32–44.

_____. "Race of Experimenter in Racial Attitude Measurement." *Psychological Reports* (1972d), 30: 771–774.

_____. "Measuring Racial Attitudes of White Males and Females." Paper presented at National Council on Measurement in Education Convention, New Orleans, Feb. 28, 1973a.

_____. "Racism and Research: Using Data to Initiate Change." *Personnel and Guidance Journal* (1973b), 52: 184–188.

_____. "Predictors of Academic Success for University Students in Special Programs." *Journal of Nonwhite Concerns in Personnel and Guidance* (1976).

————, and Chaples, E. A. "Problems in Measuring Racial Attitudes: An Experimental Approach." *Cultural Study Center Research Report No. 11–71,* University of Maryland, 1971. Also presented at the National Council on Measurement in Education Convention, Chicago, April, 1972.

Sedlacek, W. E., Brooks, G. C., Jr., Christensen, K. C., Harway, M., and Merritt, M. S. "Racism and Sexism: A Comparison and Contrast." *Journal of the National Association of Women Deans, Administrators and Counselors* (1976).

Sedlacek, W. E., Brooks, G. C., Jr., and Herman, M. H. "Black Student Attitudes Toward a Predominantly White University." *Cultural Study Center Research Report No. 8–71,* University of Maryland, 1971.

Sedlacek, W. E., Brooks, G. C., Jr., and Horowitz, J. L. "Black Admissions to Large Universities: Are Things Changing?" *Journal of College Student Personnel* (1972), 13: 305–310.

Sedlacek, W. E., Brooks, G. C., Jr., and Mindus, L. A. "Black and Other Minority Admissions to Large Universities: Three Year National Trends." *Journal of College Student Personnel* (1973a), 14: 16–21.

————. "Racial Attitudes of White University Students and Their Parents." *Cultural Study Center Research Report No. 2–73,* University of Maryland, 1973. Also in *Journal of College Student Personnel* (1973b), 14: 517–520.

Sedlacek, W. E., and Horowitz, J. L. "Changing Perceptions: An Individual or Environmental Approach." *Journal of the National Association of Student Personnel Administrators* (1974), 11: 48–51.

Sedlacek, W. E., Lewis, J. A., and Brooks, G. C., Jr. "Black and Other Minority Admissions to Large Universities: A Four Year National Survey of Policies and Outcomes." *Research in Higher Education* (1974), 2: 227–230.

Sedlacek, W. E., Merritt, M.S., and Brooks, G. C., Jr. "A National Comparison of Universities Successful and Unsuccessful in Enrolling Blacks over a Five Year Period." *Journal of College Student Personnel* (1975), 16: 57–63.

Sheriff, M., and Sheriff, C. W. *Readings in Attitude Theory and Measurement.* New York: Wiley, 1967.

Shockley, W. "Negro IQ and Heredity." *School and Society* (1969), 96: 127–128.

Silberman, C. E. *Crisis in Black and White.* New York: Vintage, 1964.

————. *Crisis in the Classroom: The Remaking of American Education.* New York: Random House, 1970.

Sizemore, B. A. "Separatism: A Reality Approach to Inclusion." In R. L. Green, *Racial Crisis in American Education.* Chicago: Follett, 1969.

Skinner, B. F. *Beyond Freedom and Dignity.* New York: Knopf, 1971.

Smith, E. B. *The Death of Slavery: The United States, 1837–65.* Chicago: University of Chicago Press, 1967.

Spence, J. T., and Helmreich, R. "The Attitudes Toward Women Scale: An Objective Instrument to Measure Attitudes Toward the Rights and Roles of Women in Contemporary Society." *Journal Supplement Abstract Service* (1972), 2: 66.

Stanley, J. C. "Predicting College Success of the Educationally Disadvantaged." *Science* (1971), 171: 640–647.

————, and Porter, A. C. "Correlation of Scholastic Aptitude Test Scores with College Grades for Negroes versus Whites." *Journal of Educational Measurement* (1967), 4: 199–218.

Thomas, C. L., and Stanley, J. C. "Effectiveness of High School Grades for Predicting College Grades of Black Students: A Review and Discussion." *Journal of Educational Measurement* (1969), 6: 203–215.

Thomas, C. V., and Comer, M. P. "Racism and Mental Health Services." In C. V. Willie, B. M. Kramer, and B. S. Brown, *Racism and Mental Health.* Pittsburgh: University of Pittsburgh Press, 1973.

Tittle, C. R., and Hill, R. J. "Attitude Measurement and the Prediction of Behavior: An Evaulation of Conditions and Measurement Techniques." *Sociometry* (1967), 30: 199–213.

Toffler, A. *Future Shock*. New York: Bantam, 1970.

Triandis, H. C. *The Analysis of Subjective Culture*. New York: Wiley, 1972.

Troy, W. G., Sedlacek, W. E., and Chapman, T. H. "An Evaluation of Three Methods of Racism—Sexism Training in a University Student Orientation Program." *Cultural Study Center Research Report No. 1–75,* University of Maryland, 1975.

U.S. Commission on Civil Rights. *Your Child and Busing*. Washington, D.C.: U.S. Government Printing Office, 1972.

Vontress, C. E. "Counseling Negro Students for College." *Journal of Negro Education* (1968), 37: 34–44.

Warner, L. G., and DeFleur, M. L. "Attitudes as an Interactional Concept: Social Constraint and Social Distance as Intervening Variables Between Attitudes and Action." *American Sociological Review* (1969), 34: 153–169.

Watts, W., and Free, L. A. *State of the Nation*. New York: Universe Books, 1973.

Webster's New Collegiate Dictionary. Springfield, Mass.: G. & C. Merriam Co., 1973.

Weissburg, N. C. "On DeFleur and Wester's Attitude as a Scientific Concept." *Social Forces* (1965), 43: 422.

Weisstein, N. "Psychology Constructs the Female; or the Fantasy Life of the Male Psychologist (with Some Attention to the Fantasies of His Friends, the Male Biologist and the Male Anthropologist)." *Social Education* (1971), 35: 362–373.

Whaples, G. C. "The Situational Attitude Scale (SAS) as an Attitude Measurement Tool for Adults Involved in Extension 4-H and Youth Programs." *4-H Intern Report No. 3–74.* Washington, D.C.: U.S. Department of Agriculture, 1974.

Williams, F., Whitehead, J., and Miller, L. *Attitudinal Correlates of Children's Speech Characteristics*. Final Report, No. 00336, Grant No. OEGO–70–7868 (508). Washington, D.C.: U.S. Government Printing Office, 1971.

Yette, S. F. *The Choice*. New York: Putnam, 1971.

Name Index

Adams, M., 173, 205
Adorno, T. W., 70, 205
Alinsky, S. D., 111, 112, 113,
    152, 154, 155, 205
Allport, G. W., 19, 38, 205
Amir, Y., 92, 205
Attucks, C., 182

Baird, L. L., 50, 205
Ball, H. W., 71, 205
Banks, J. A., 94, 206
Baratz, J. C., 24, 25, 206
Barbanel, L., 206
Barney, P. O., 60, 206
Bashook, P., 208
Beattie, M., 15, 55, 210
Belcher, L., 59, 210
Berger, S. E., 20, 206
Birk, J. M., 164, 206
Bravy, S., 179
Brooke, E., 185
Brooks, G. C., Jr., 15, 17, 51,
    52, 54, 55, 56, 60, 61, 64,
    66, 67, 69, 70, 71, 72, 73,
93, 122, 163, 175, 206,
    207, 208, 209, 211, 212,
    213, 214, 215
Brooks, L., 206
Brown, B. S., 216
Brown, J., 185

Campbell, E. Q., 208
Carrington, C., 179
Carroll, P., 179
Carver, G. W., 182
Chaples, E. A., 64, 70, 206, 207
Chapman, T. H., 46, 48, 160,
    161, 174, 175, 207, 217
Chesler, M. A., 125, 207
Christensen, K. C., 59, 165,
    175, 207, 215
Clark, K. B., 42, 51, 207
Clarke, J., 179
Cleary, T. A., 51, 207
Cleaver, E., 19, 208
Cobbs, P. M., 16, 19, 210
Cole, N. S., 59, 208
Coleman, J. S., 127, 208

Collins, A. M., 165, 208
Comer, J. P., 16, 208
Comer, M. P., 38, 216
Culbertson, F. M., 82, 208

Daniels, R., 38, 40, 208
D'Costa, A., 50, 59, 208
DeFleur, M. L., 92, 208, 217
Deutsch, M., 213
DiCesare, A., 15, 54, 55, 56,
    60, 208
Disch, R., 37, 40, 213
Dove, 27, 28
Downs, A., 44, 115, 208
Dreger, R. M., 211, 213

Eberly, C. G., 71, 209
Ehrlich, H. J., 38, 209
Elliott, P., 208
Ellison, R., 60, 209
Epps, E. G., 54, 209

Fago, D. P., 179
Farquhar, W. W., 51, 210
Farver, A. S., 51, 52, 209
Fendrich, J. M., 92, 209
Franklin, J. H., 17, 209
Free, L. A., 176, 217
Frenkel-Brunswik, E., 205

Gardner, J. L., 165, 209
Gardner, J. W., 113, 114, 115,
    139, 209
Glock, C. Y., 38, 42, 94, 209,
    211
Golden, H., 13, 210
Gordy, B., 185
Gossett, T. F., 41, 210
Green, R. L., 51, 60, 210
Grier, W. H., 16, 19, 210
Gurin, G., 15, 55, 56, 210
Gurin, P., 15, 55, 56, 210

Hall, L. D., 60, 206
Handley, A., 179
Hanson, G. R., 59, 210
Hartnagel, T. F., 19, 210

Harway, M., 175, 215
Hedman, A. R., 161, 210
Helmreich, R., 174, 216
Henry, J., 189
Herman, M. H., 46, 71, 164,
    167, 206, 210, 215
Hernton, C. C., 19, 211
Hesburgh, T. M., 38, 211
Hill, R. J., 92, 216
Hitler, 125, 185
Hobson, C. J., 208
Horowitz, J. L., 52, 72, 122,
    211, 215
Horton, C. P., 127, 213
Hyman, H. H., 92, 211

Jackson, J. J., 19, 211
Jackson, M., 185, 199
Jackson, W. L., 29
Jacobson, L., 59, 213
Jamal, A., 29
Janis, I. L., 82, 211
Jarecky, R., 208
Jensen, A. R., 42, 211, 213
John, A., 29
Johnson, K. R., 25, 211
Jones, F., 29
Jones, L., 29
Juhasz, J., 206

Katz, I., 213
King, B. T., 82, 211
King, M. L., 34
Kitano, H. H. L., 38, 40, 208
Knowles, L. L., 37, 211
Kramer, B. M., 216

Ladwig, G. W., 20, 211
Lao, R., 15, 55, 210
Leavell, W., 208
Lee, P., 30
Lefcourt, H. M., 20, 211
Leitner, D. W., 70, 211
Levinson, D. J., 205
Lewis, J. A., 61, 71, 212, 215
Linn, R. L., 59, 212

McDougal, W., 29
McPartland, J., 208
Maehr, M. L., 59, 212
Maslow, A. H., 2, 212
Merritt, M. S., 93, 175, 212, 215
Miller, K. S., 211, 213
Miller, L., 24, 217
Mindus, L., 52, 69, 93, 207, 215
Miyares, J., 179
Mood, A. M., 208
Moynihan, D. P., 19, 212

Nader, R., 114, 212
Noar, G., 27, 212
Nobers, D. R., 19, 212

Parker, C., 30
Pfeifer, C. M., Jr., 16, 51, 52, 212
Plotkin, L., 51, 207
Pocahontas, 40
Polo, M., 40
Porter, A. C., 16, 216
Prewitt, K., 37, 211
Prieto, D., 208

Rayder, N. F., 60, 207
Roberts, S. O., 127, 213
Rokeach, M., 70, 213
Rolfe, J., 40
Rosenthal, R., 59, 213
Rothenberg, P. J., 20, 213
Rovner, R., 71, 213
Rubovits, P. C., 59, 213

Sanford, R. N., 205
Schwartz, B. N., 37, 40, 213
Sedlacek, W. E., 15, 16, 17, 45, 46, 51, 52, 54, 55, 56, 59, 60, 61, 64, 66, 67, 69, 70, 71, 72, 73, 93, 120, 122, 161, 163, 164, 165, 167, 175, 206, 207, 208, 209, 210, 211, 212, 213, 214, 215, 217
Seltzer, R. A., 206

Sheriff, C. W., 39, 216
Sheriff, M., 39, 216
Shockley, W., 42, 216
Siegelman, E., 38, 42, 94, 209, 211
Silberman, C. E., 59, 94, 216
Sizemore, B. A., 22, 216
Skinner, B. F., 44, 45, 216
Smith, E. B., 41, 216
Spence, J. T., 174, 216
Stanley, J. C., 16, 50, 51, 216
Stark, R., 42, 209
Stevenson, J., 179
Strader, M., 52, 215

Tangri, S. S., 55, 206
Tedeschi, J. T., 20, 206
Thomas, C. L., 51, 216
Thomas, C. V., 38, 216
Thrush, R., 59, 210
Tittle, C. R., 92, 216
Toffler, A., 3, 217
Triandis, H. C., 14, 217
Troy, W. G., 161, 179, 217

Vontress, C. E., 60, 217

Warner, L. G., 92, 217
Washington, B. T., 34
Watts, W., 176, 217
Weinfield, F. D., 208
Weissburg, N. C., 92, 217
Weisstein, N., 163, 217
Wester, F. R., 92, 208, 217
Whaples, G. C., 71, 217
Whitehead, J., 24, 217
Williams, F., 24, 217
Williams, R. L., 27
Williams, R. O., 179
Willie, C. V., 216
Wright, L. M., 179

Yette, S. F., 23, 217
York, R. L., 208
Young, L., 30

Subject Index

Admissions policies, 6, 50–59,
116–18
African ancestry, 20, 21
Alcoholism, as analogous to
racism, 7, 62
American College Test (ACT),
51
Association of American
Medical Colleges, 50, 59
Attitudinal racism, 38–39, 43,
63–80
Attrition, 25, 57
Authoritarian scale of Adorno,
et al., relationship with
SAS, 70–71
Authority, reactions to, 5, 26

Behavior change: criteria for
measuring, 3, 10, 68, 105,
145, 159–77; goals, 8–9, 94,
97–106, 144–45, 151;
strategies for

accomplishing, 8–9, 93–94,
98, 107–34, 136–39,
144–45, 151, 157–58
Behavioral racism, 2, 6, 42–46,
86
Black, connotations of the word,
40
Black Intelligence Test of
Cultural Homogeneity
(BITCH), 27
Blacks: dialect, 5, 8, 11, 16,
24–25, 105, 131–32; role in
eliminating racism, 135–45;
views of race and racism,
15, 22–23, 55, 117–18,
135–45
Busing, 103, 125–27

Campus Coalition Against
Racism (University of
Maryland), 99
Change. See Behavior change

223

Change agent, 4, 9, 20, 99–100, 108–15, 118, 120–22, 127, 135–45, 147–58
Chicanos, 12, 24
Christianity, relationship of to racism, 40–42
Common Cause, 113–15
Compromise, 9, 121
Constitution, of U.S., 110
Consultants, role of in combating racism: the black consultant, 135–47; the white consultant, 147–58
Cultural and racial differences, 5, 10–35, 140–41, 148–49
Cultural and racial identity, 5, 21, 23, 140
Cultural assimilation, 21
Cultural pluralism, 14
Cultural-racial groups, 12–13, 21–22, 26–27, 162
Cultural Study Center, University of Maryland, 53, 115–16, 119–20
Culture, definition of, 11–12
Curriculum: elementary and secondary, 8–9, 48–49, 94–95, 100, 103, 106, 123–24, 134; higher education, 6, 60–61, 118–19, 123–24, 134

Desegregation, 103, 124–27
Dialect, 5, 8, 11, 16, 24–25, 105, 131–32
Differences, cultural and racial, 5, 10–35, 140–41, 148–49
Dogmatism Scale of Rokeach, relationship of with SAS, 70–71
Dove Counterbalance Intelligence Test ("chitlin'" test), 27–34, 178

Education. *See* Higher education; School systems
Education and Racism course, University of Maryland, 119
Elementary education. *See* School systems
Ends justifying means, 109
Ethnocentrism, 38

Family structure, 19–20

Goals in eliminating racism, examples of, 102–6

Heritage, cultural and racial, 20–21
Hierarchy of needs (Maslow), 2
Higher education: admissions policies, 6, 50–59, 116–18; counseling programs, 60, 118, 133; curriculum, 6, 60–61, 118–19, 123–24, 134; environmental supports for, 25, 52, 56–57, 129; extracurricular activities, 6, 60; faculty and staff, 6, 59–61, 122–23, 139; funding, 7, 61; prediction of academic performance, 50–59
History of racism, 39–42
Homosexuality, 163
Hostility, 26
Human relations programs, 49, 101, 103, 133–34, 138–39

Identity, cultural and racial, 5, 21, 23, 140
Immigrant groups, 21
Indians, American, 12, 40, 152–55
Individual racism, 5, 45–46, 110–11, 143
Institutional racism, 5, 43, 45–47, 55–56, 62, 98, 102,

110–11, 116–17, 139, 143

Integrity, 151

Jews, 12

Language. *See* Dialect
Law School Admissions Council, 50
Leadership ability, 57–58

Marriage, interracial, 40
Matriarchy, 19
Meet the Bureaucracy game, 174–75
Melting pot, 14
Mexican American, 12, 24
Minority groups: definition of, 13–14; self-concept, 13, 22, 53–56

National Advisory Commission on Civil Disorders, 37
National Scholarship Service and Fund for Negro Students, 51
Native Americans, 12, 40, 152–55
Nazi Germany, 162
Nixon, Richard, administration of, 177
Nontraditional predictors of academic performance, 53–59

Power, 9, 20, 22–23, 45, 121
Prejudice: definition of, 38–39; religious, 42. *See also* Racism
Prisoner's Dilemma game, 20
Public Interest Research Group (PIRG), 114
Puritan ethic, 41

Quotas, 102, 122

Race, definition of, 11–12
Racial and cultural differences, 5, 10–35, 140–41, 148–49
Racial and cultural identity, 5, 21, 23, 140
Racial attitudes: measurement of, 7, 63–80, 92–93; sources of, 7, 81–95, 140–44, 150–51. *See also* Situational Attitude Scale
Racial stereotypes. *See* Stereotypes
Racism: attitudinal, 38–39, 43, 63–80; behavioral, 2, 6, 42–46, 86; definition of, 2, 5–6, 14, 37–39, 44, 162; dynamics of, 5, 37–62, 142–43, 149–50; examples of, 6, 47, 55, 59–61, 116–17, 119, 141; history of, 39–42; individual, 5, 45–46, 110–11, 143; institutional, 5, 43, 45–47, 55–56, 62, 98, 102, 110–11, 116–17, 139, 143; rationalizations for, 3, 39–40; a white problem, 6, 62, 118, 141, 147–58
Reinforcement systems, 16, 20, 57
Religion, relationship to racism, 40–42, 71
Research data: race-related issues, 15–17, 20, 22, 24, 46, 51, 54–56, 59–61, 64–80, 92–93, 160–61; sex-related issues, 17, 46, 164–77; uses of, 9, 115–18, 129
Reward. *See* Reinforcement
Role playing, 82–92, 179–203

Scholastic Aptitude Test (SAT), 51, 116, 117

School systems: administration, 6, 8, 26, 47–48, 105, 132; curriculum, 8–9, 48–49, 94–95, 100, 103, 106, 123–24, 134; discipline, 8, 104, 127; funding, 6, 47; human relations programs, 49, 101, 103, 133–34, 138–39; parental involvement, 8, 10, 104–5, 129–30; programming and planning, 8, 103, 124–27; segregation of, 6, 42, 46–47; standards for judging programs, 8, 105; teachers, 6, 8–9, 16, 24, 26, 60, 95, 102–3, 122–23
Secondary education. *See* School systems
Segregation of schools, 6, 42, 46–47
Self-concept, 13, 22, 53–56
Sex roles, 16–19, 163–76
Sexism, 163–76
Situational Attitude Scale (SAS): administration of, 72–73; discussion of, 7, 46, 64–80, 92–93, 101, 129, 160; response differences between sexes, 73–74; uses of, 46, 67–72, 101, 119, 143, 150, 160
Situational Attitude Scale–Women (SAS–W), 46, 165–76
Slavery, 40–41
Social Darwinism, 41
Socio-economic factors, 19, 21, 156

Standards, admission. *See* Admissions policies
Starpower simulation game, 46, 174–75
Stereotypes: cultural and racial, 7, 16, 18, 19, 92, 93, 94, 95, 140, 141; sexual, 16–19
Strategies for eliminating racism: discussion of, 9, 107–39; evaluation of, 109; examples of, 122–34

Task Force on the Status of Women in Psychology (of APA), 164
Teachers. *See* School systems
Testing and test scores, 8, 10, 24, 50–52, 104–6, 129

United States Commission on Civil Rights, 126
University of Maryland: admissions policies, 116–18; Campus Coalition Against Racism, 99; Cultural Study Center, 53, 115–16, 119–20; Education and Racism course, 119; programs for combating racism, 116–22, 134

Vietnam war, 99

Whites: role in racism, 6, 62, 118, 141, 147–58; self-concept, 16, 147–58